I dedicate this book first to God, my source of inspiration and guide in all the journeys of my life. May your wisdom be the source of my eternal knowledge.

To my family who have always been by my side, supporting me and encouraging my goals. To you, I dedicate this book with all my love and affection.

Flávio Oliveira

2024

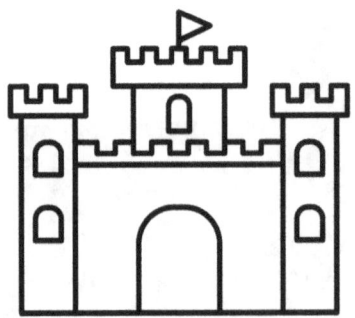
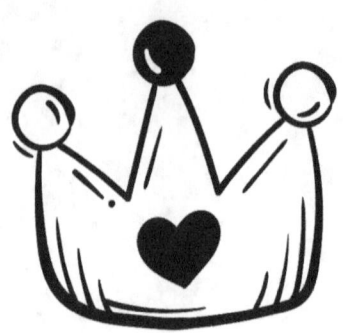

This Book Belongs to:

_____

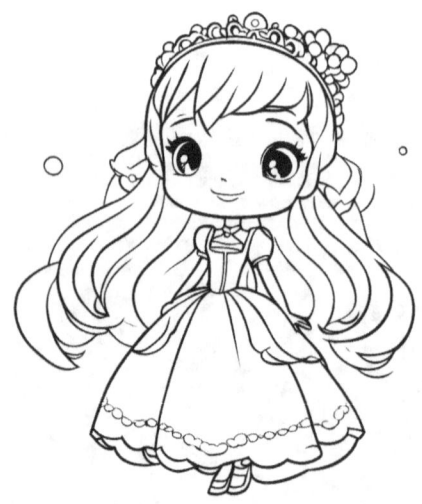
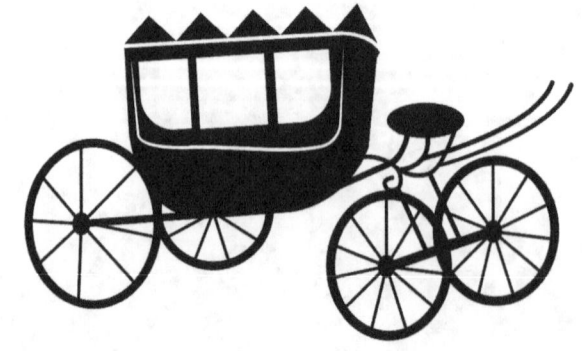

F.A. Oliveira©
all rights reserved

ALL RIGHTS RESERVED©
2024

No part of this publication may be reproduced, distributed, or transmitted in any form or by any means, including photocopying, recording, or other electronic or mechanical methods, without the prior written permission of the publisher, except for brief quotations incorporated in critical reviews and other specific noncommercial uses. Any unauthorized replica of this work is prohibited.

F.A. Oliveira©

Test Color Page

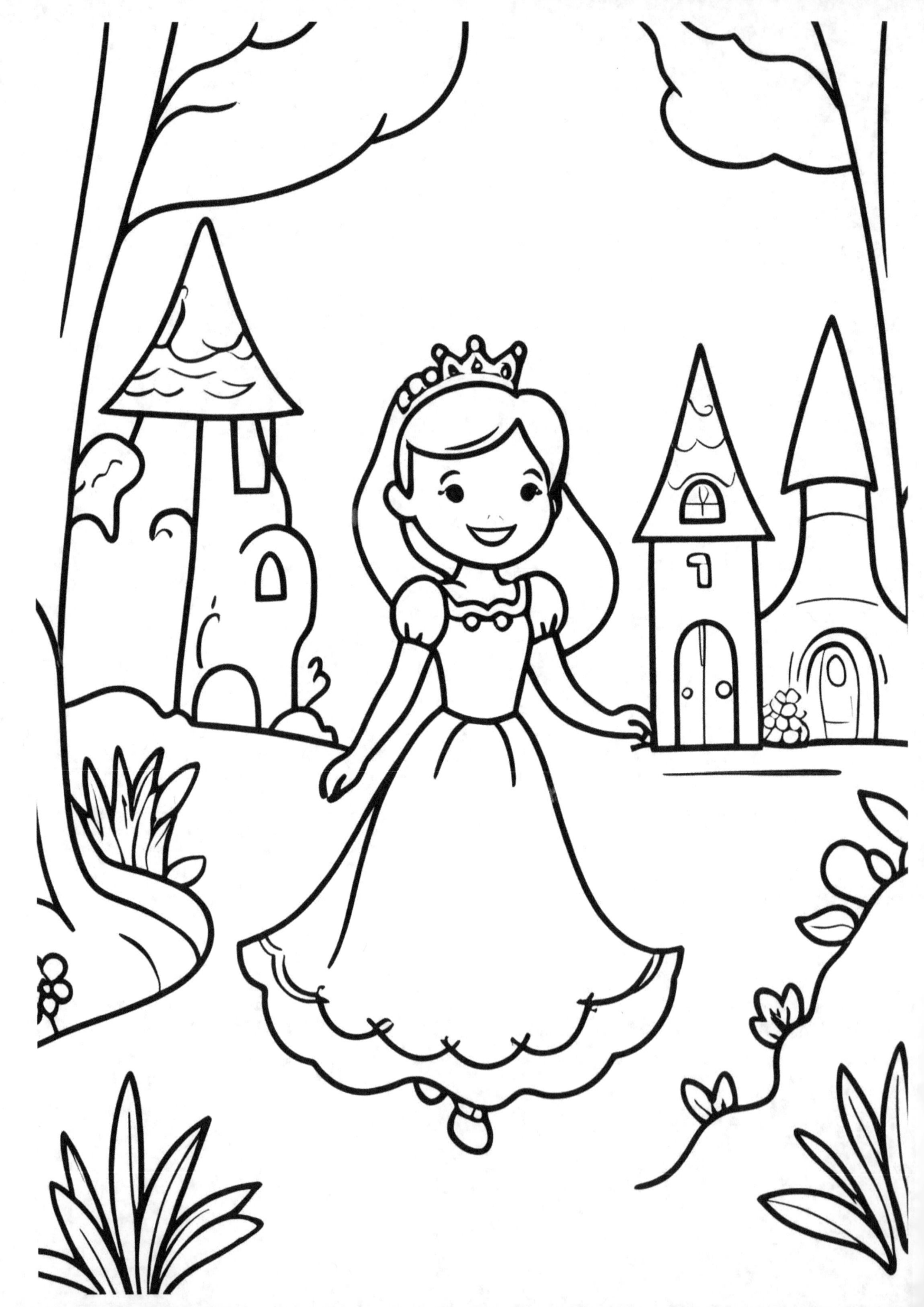

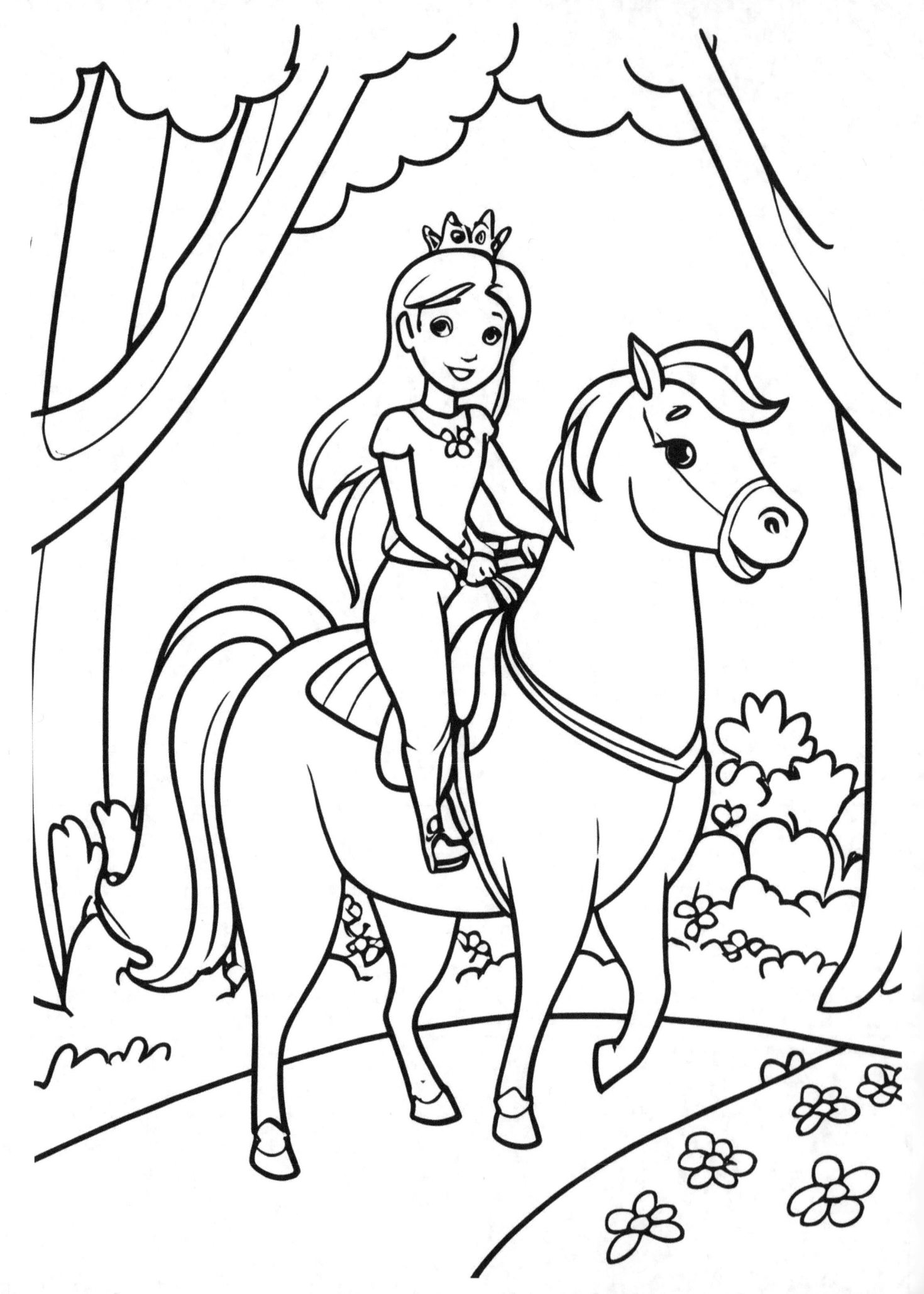

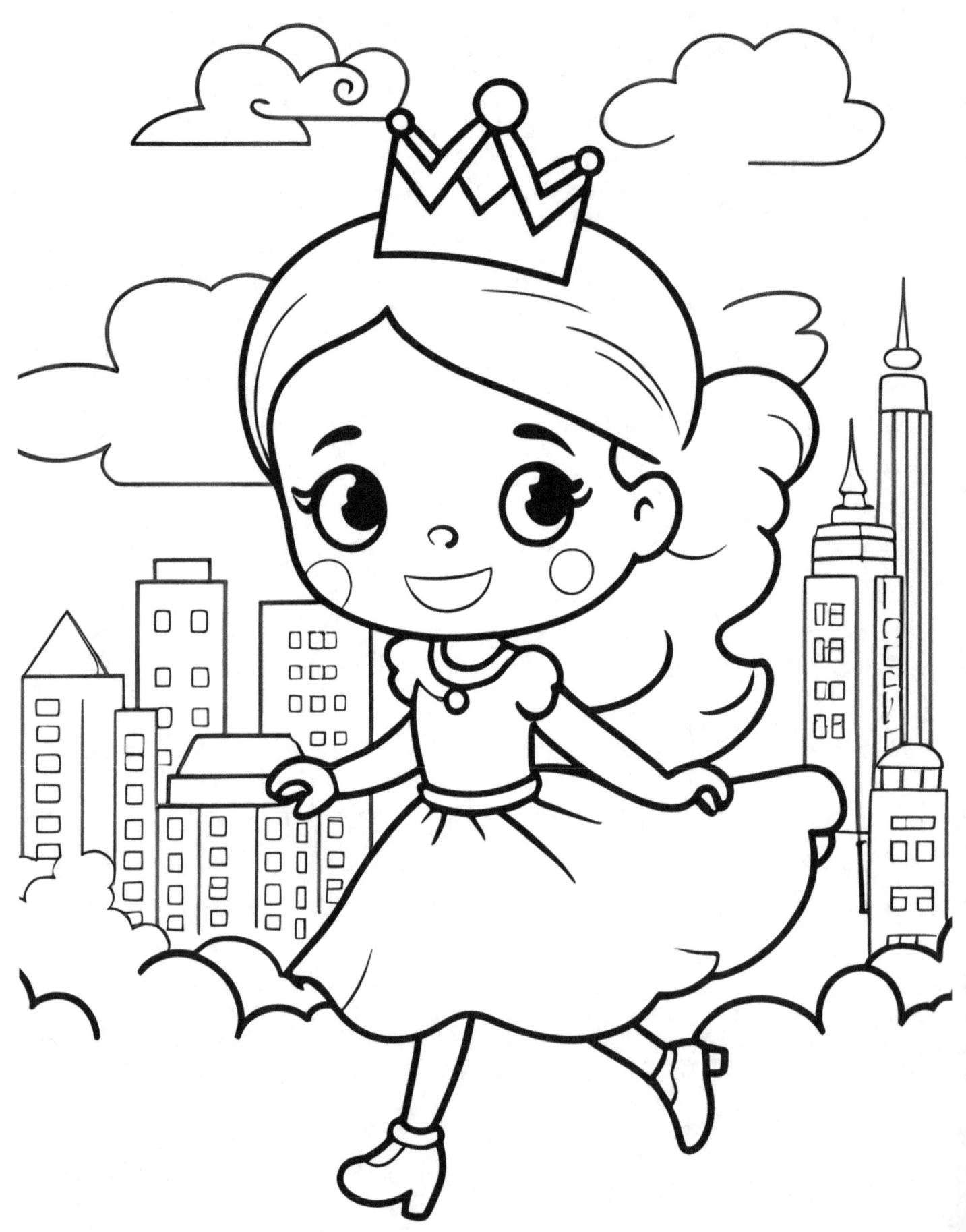

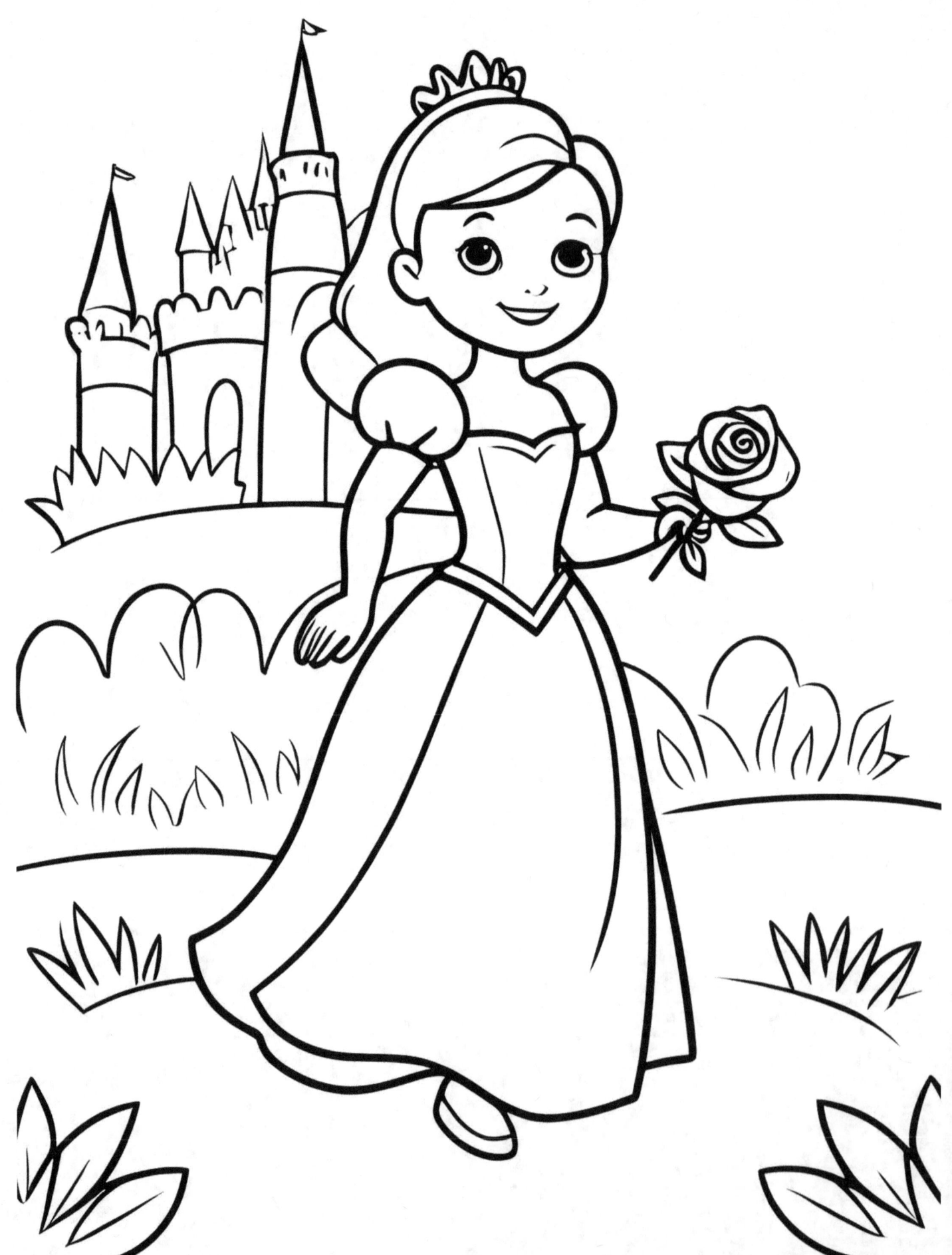

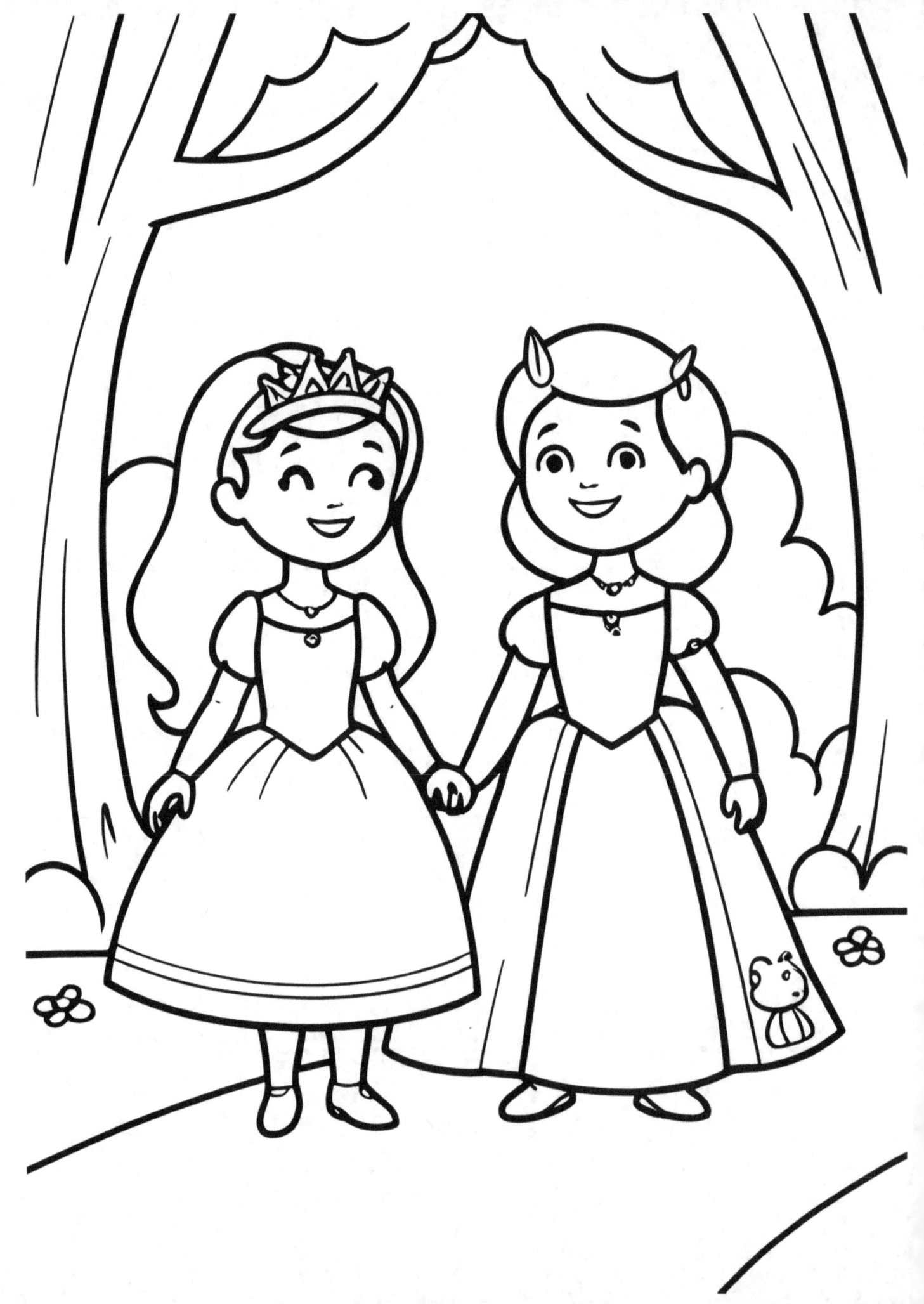

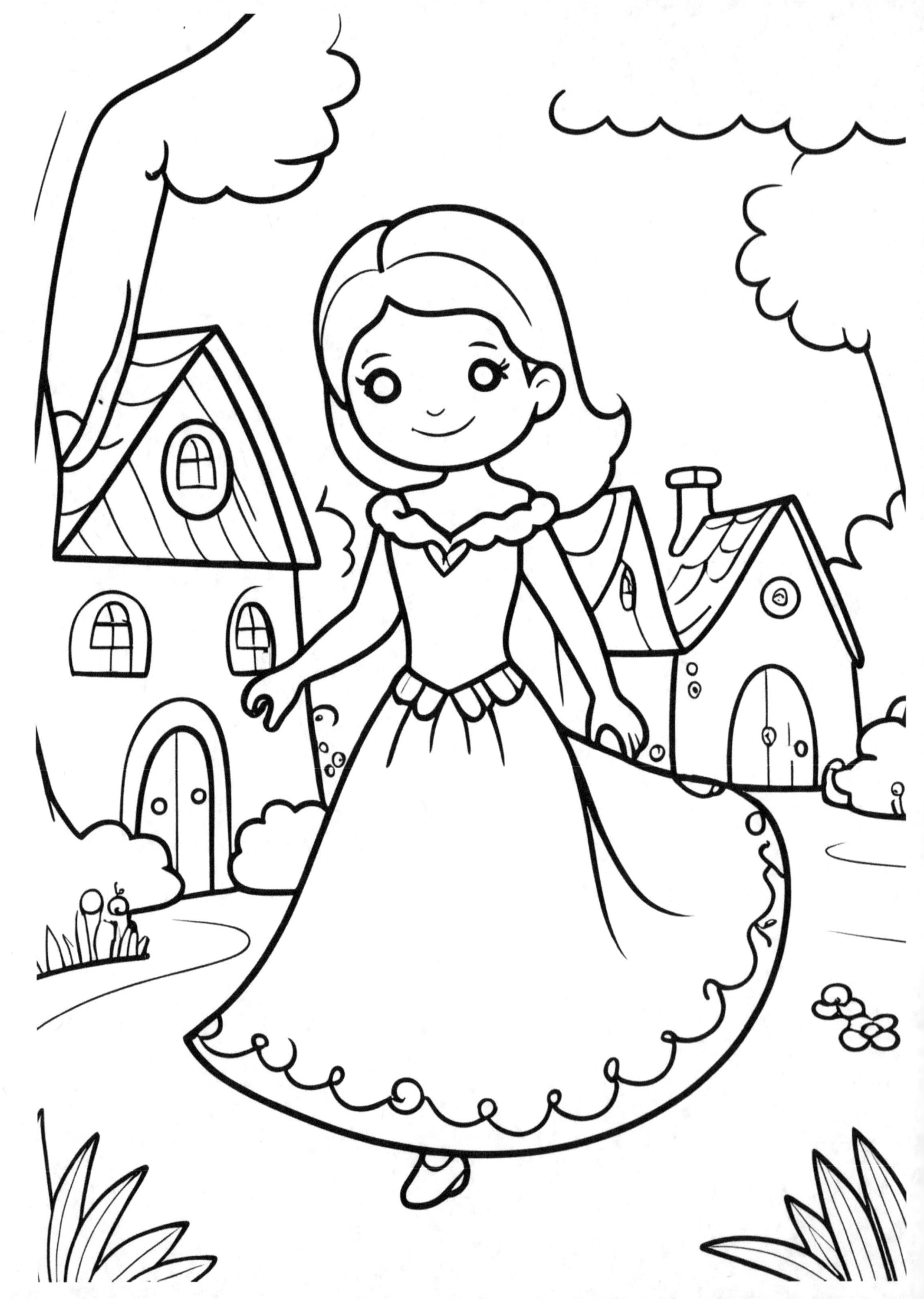

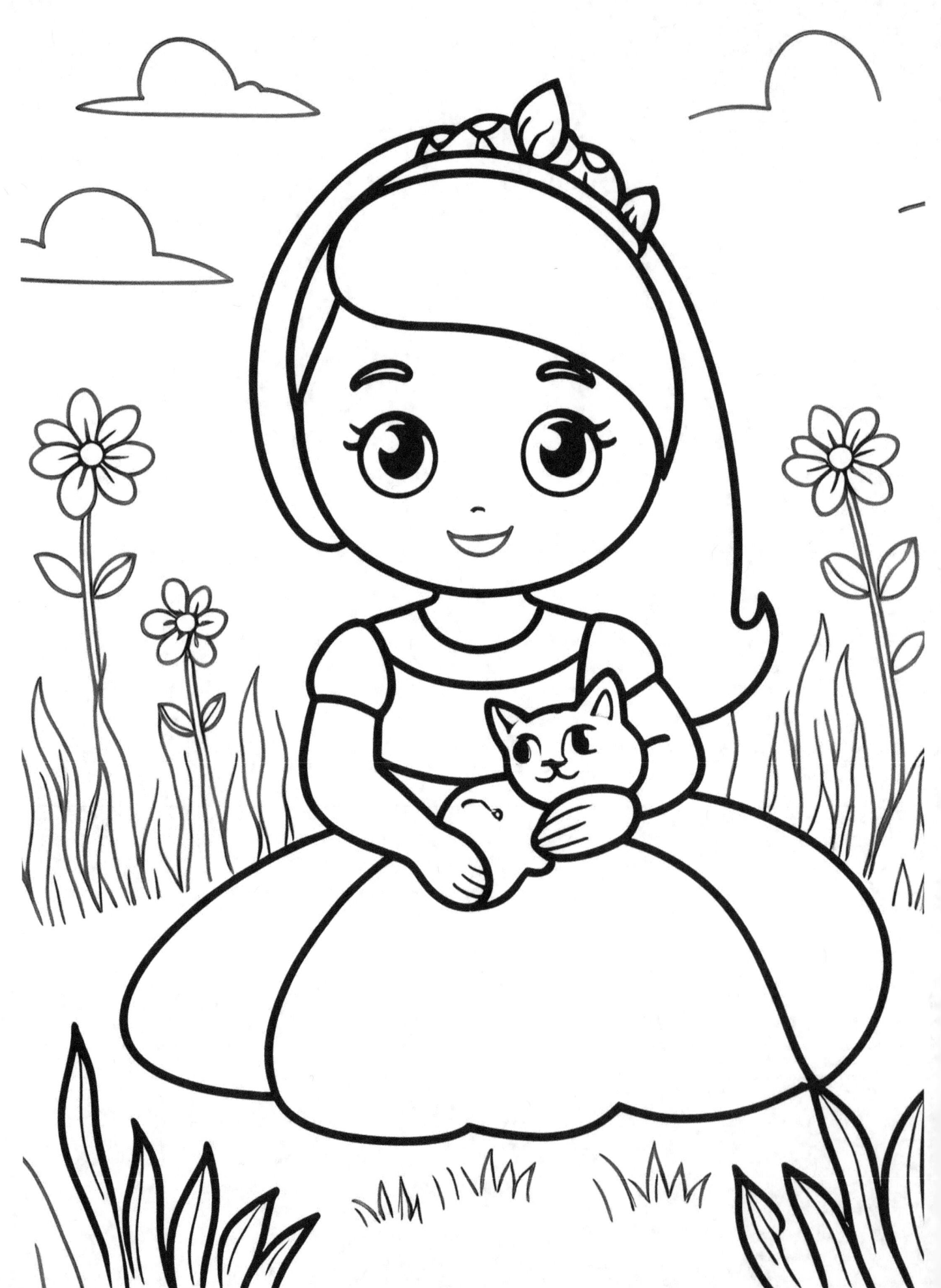

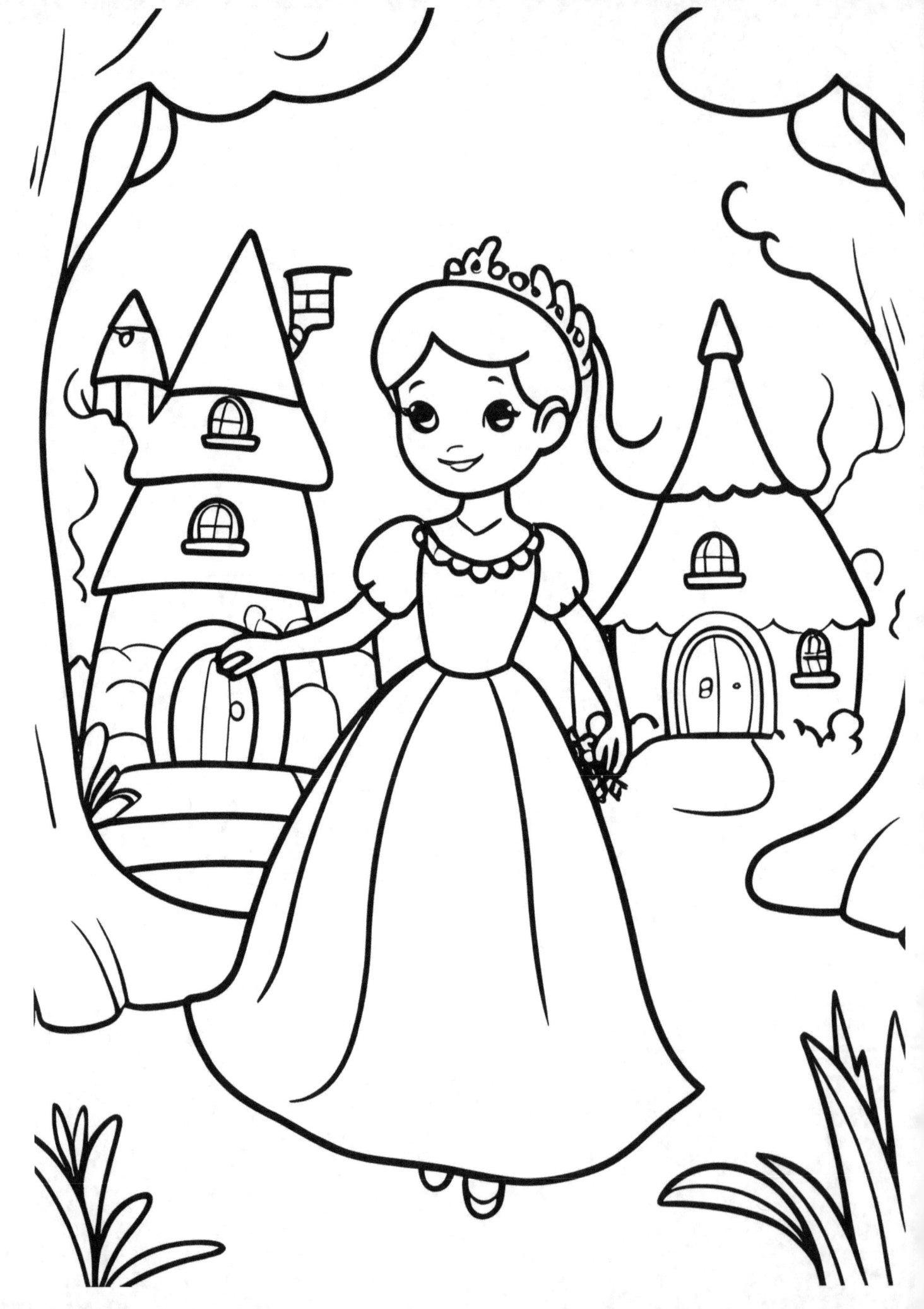

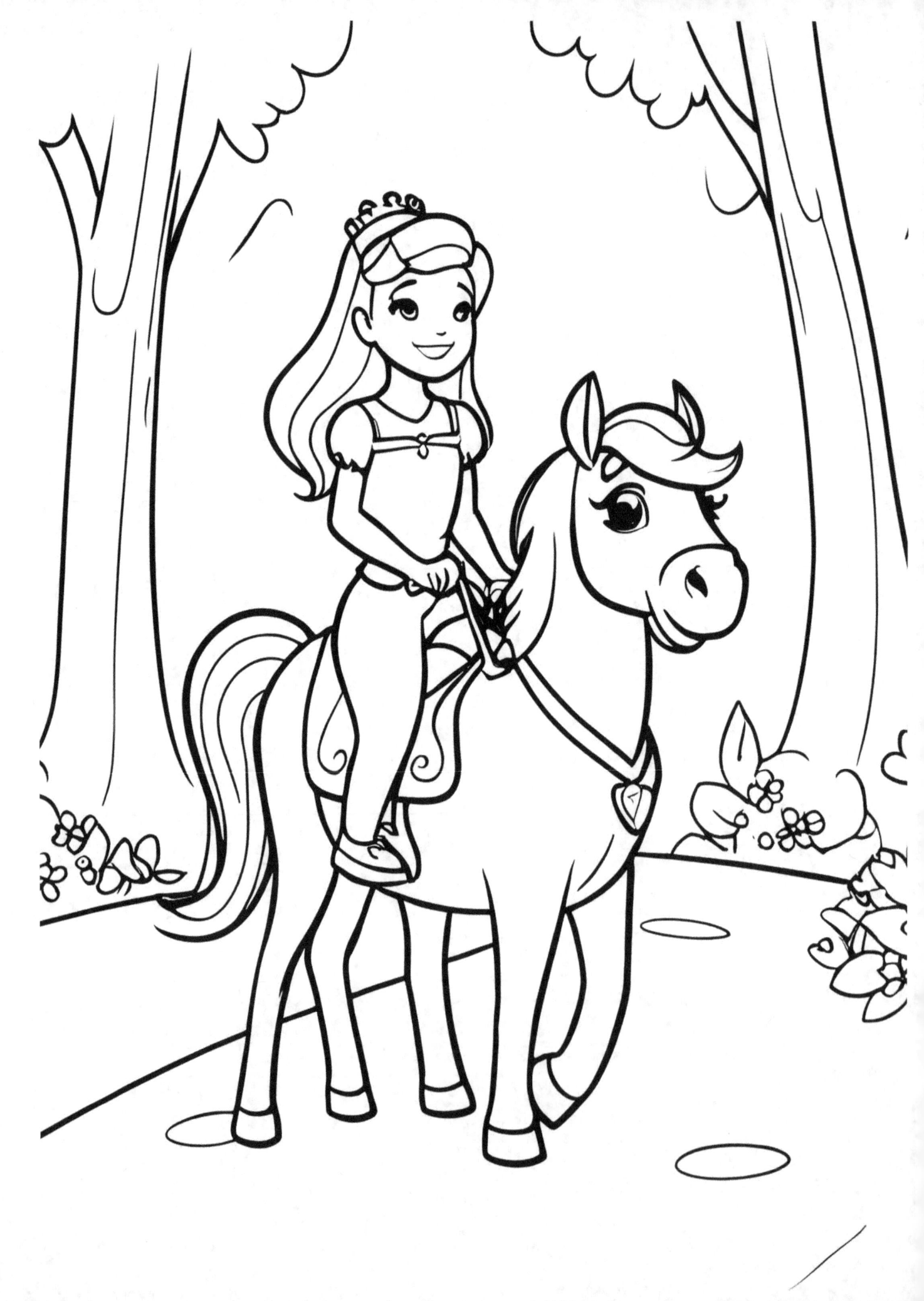

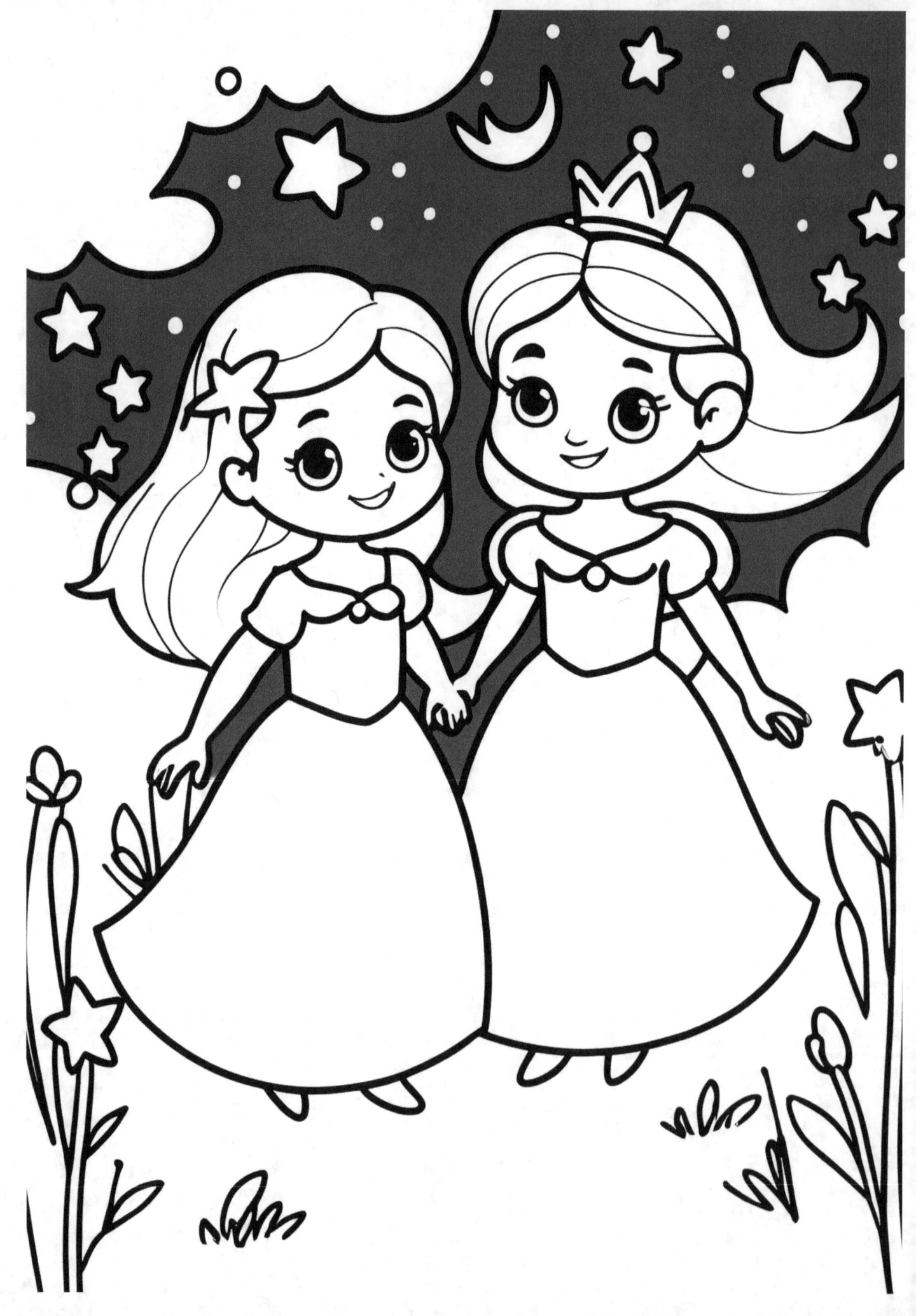

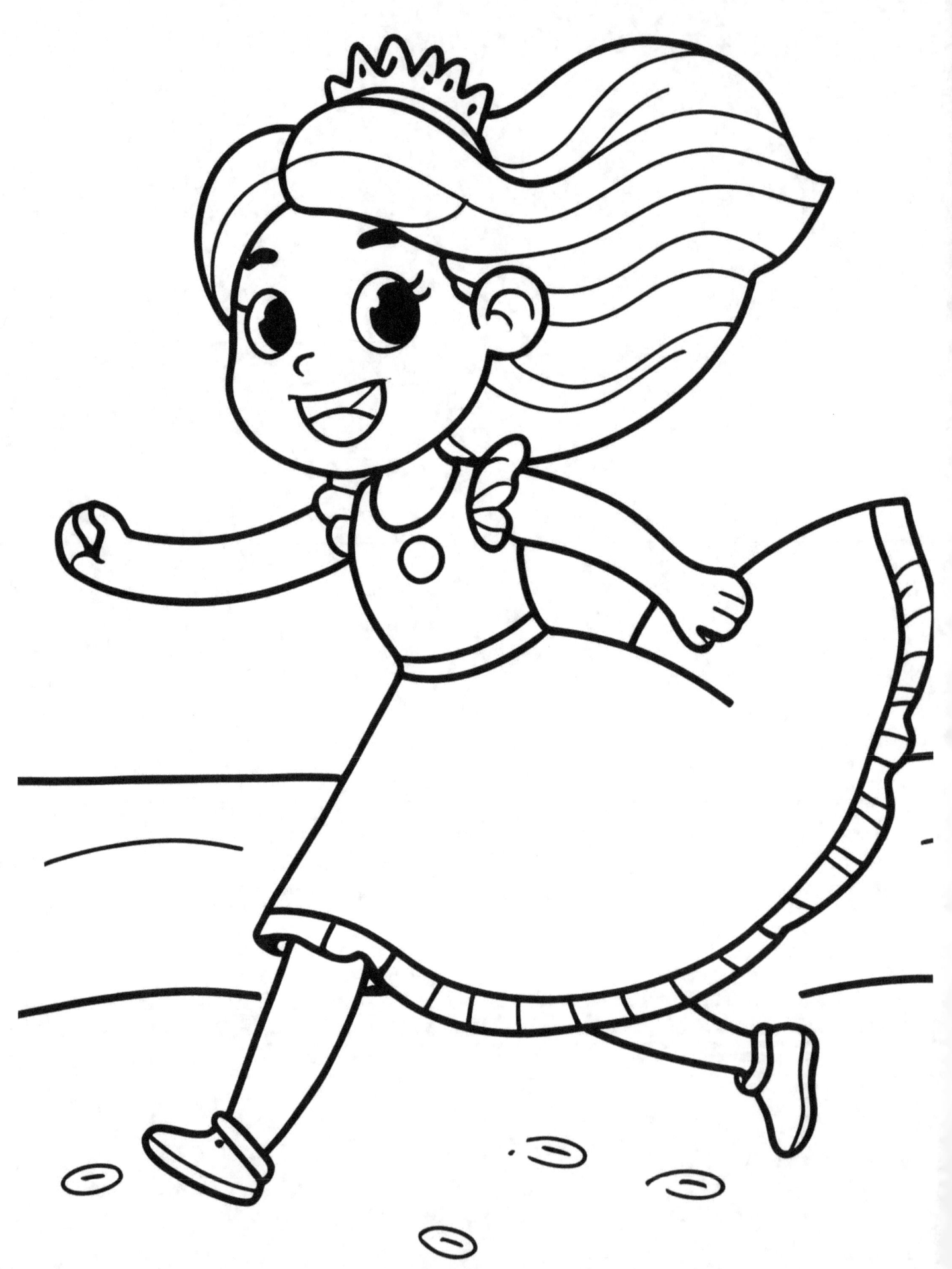

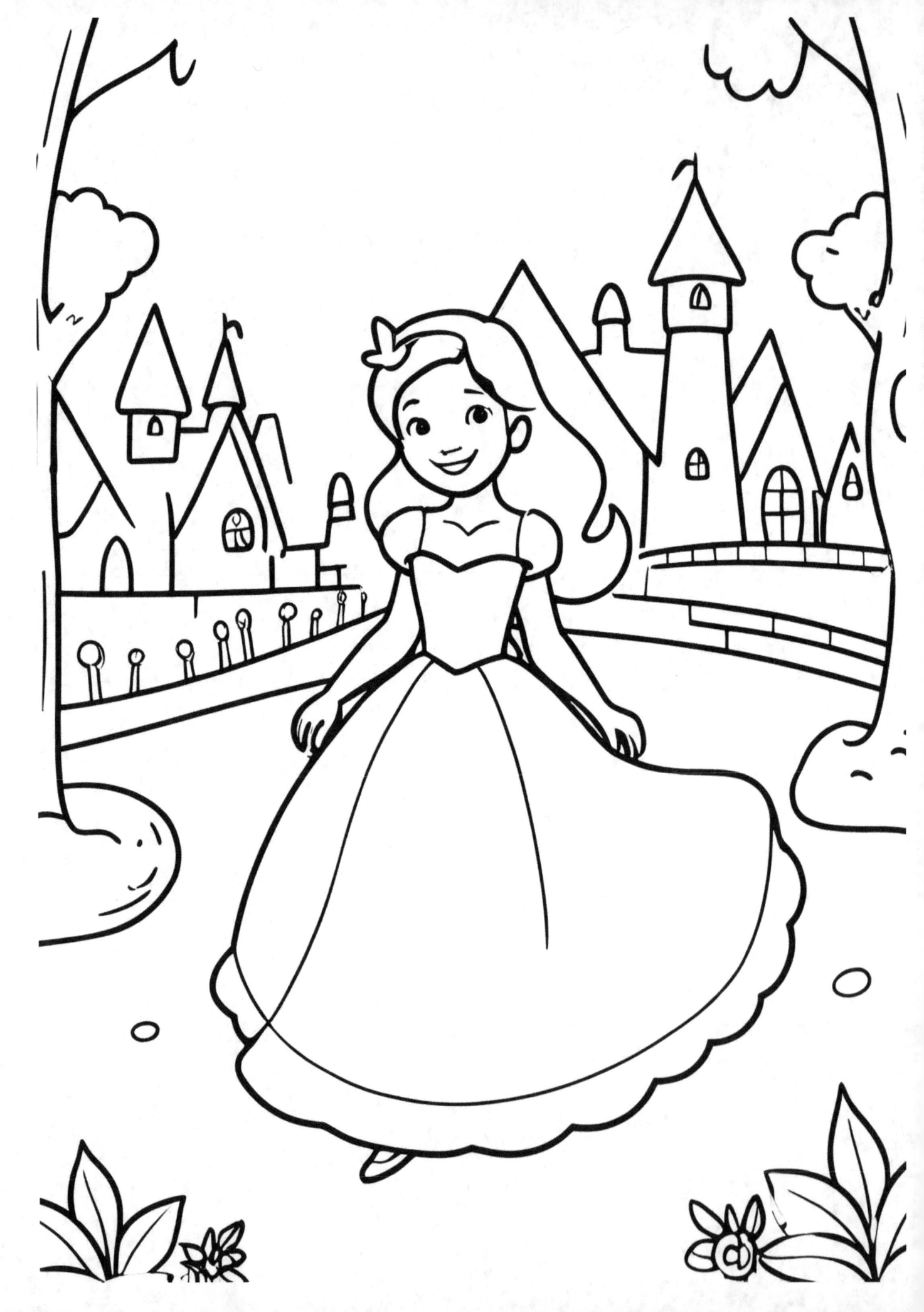

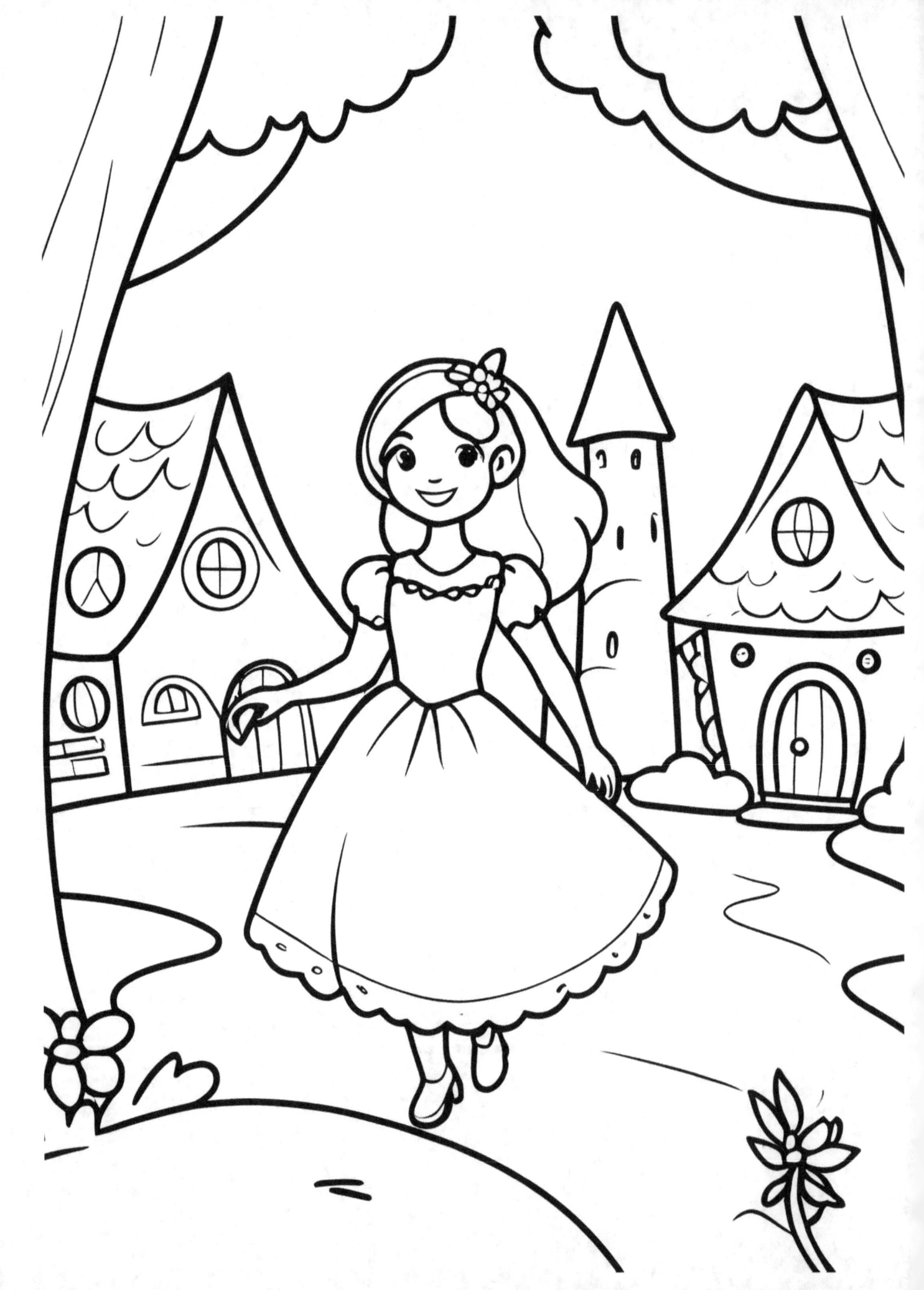

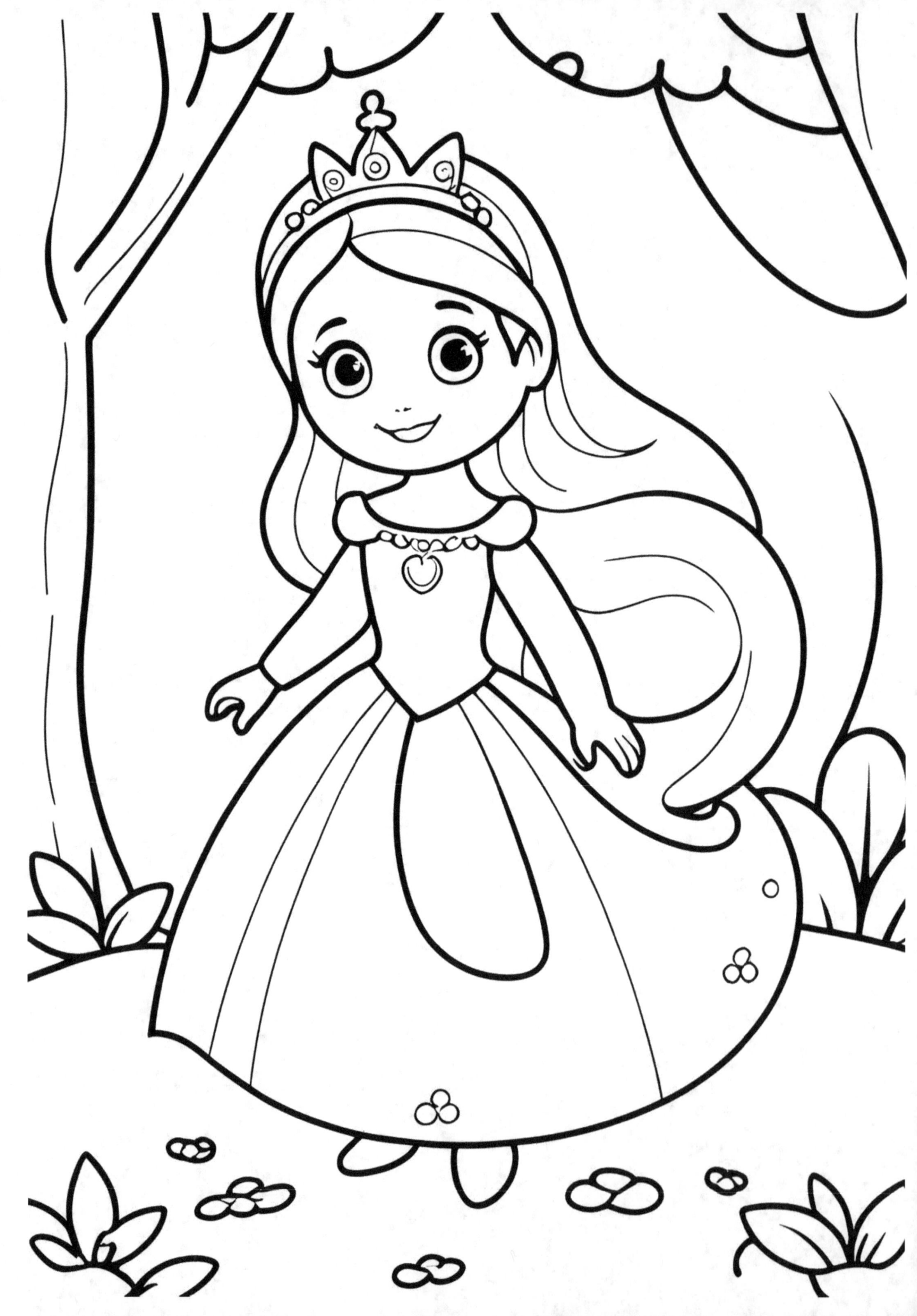

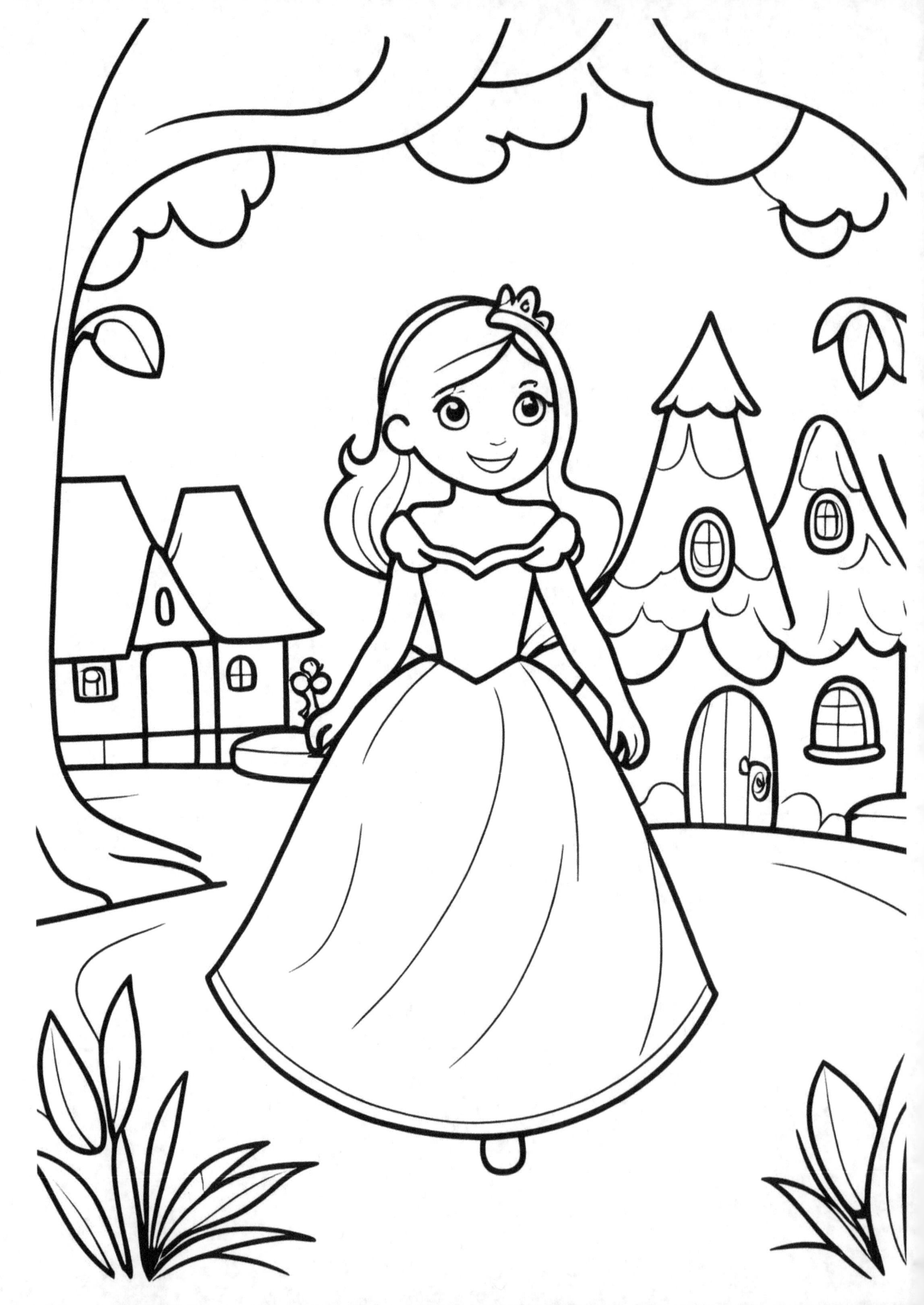

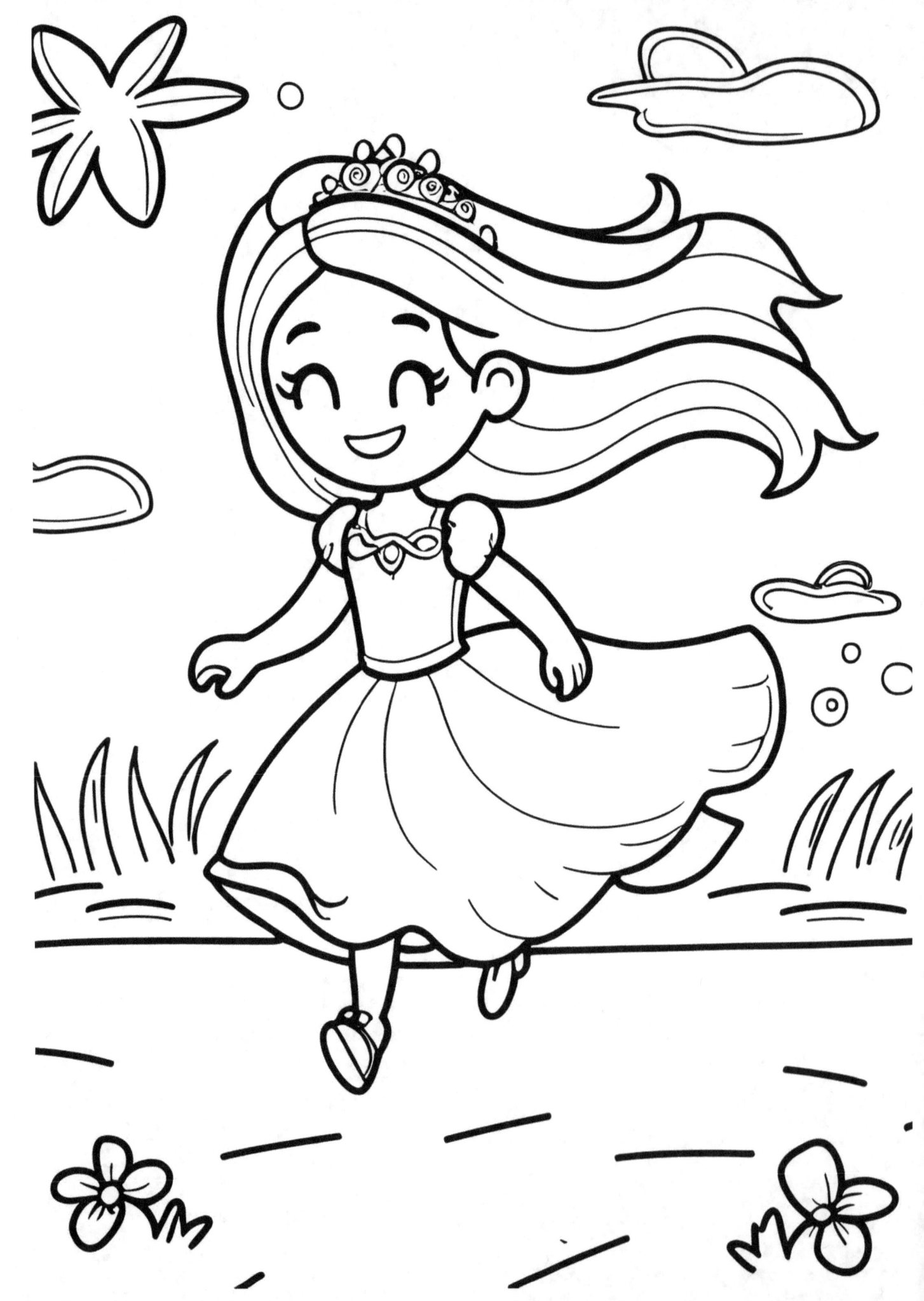

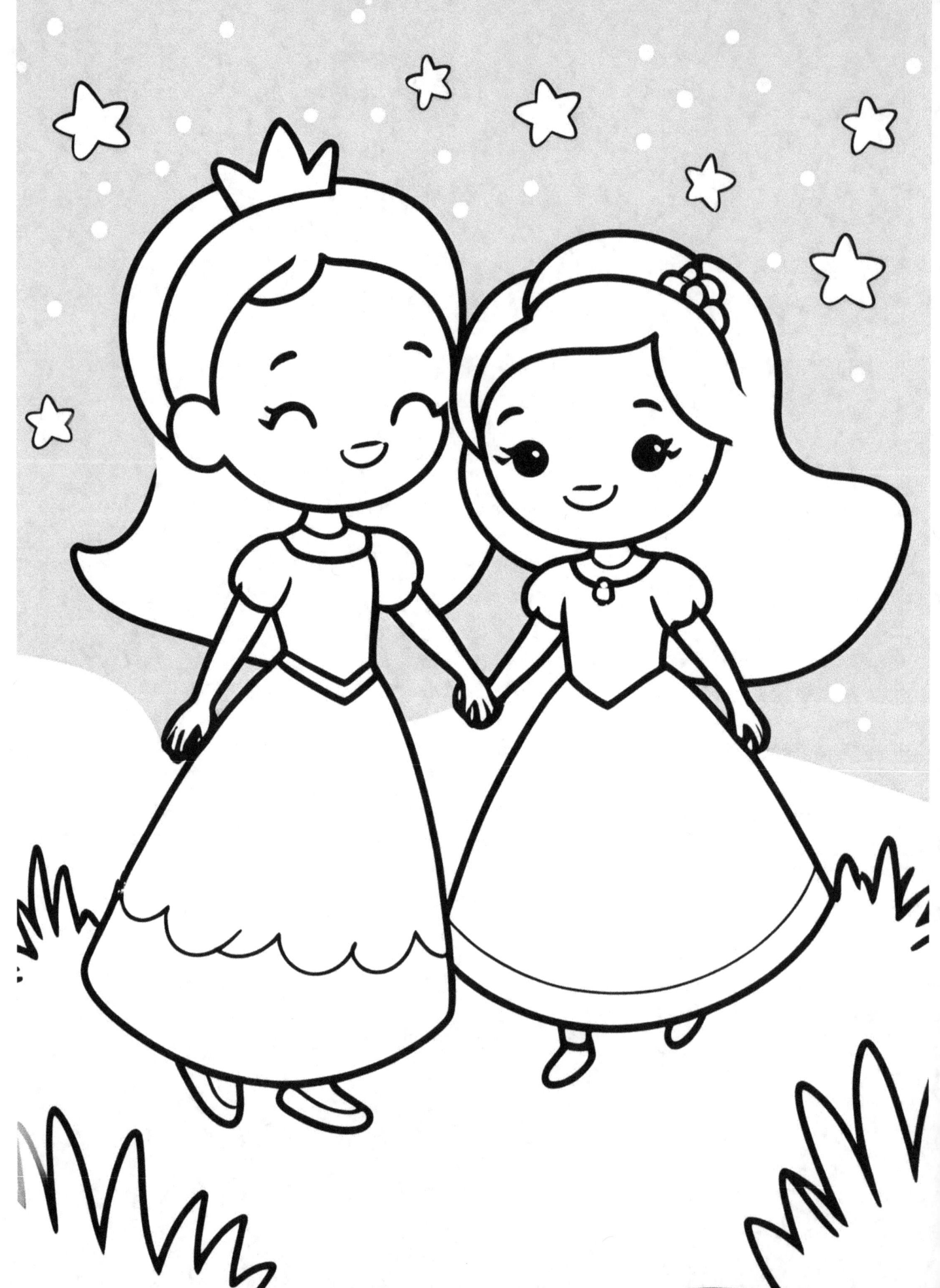

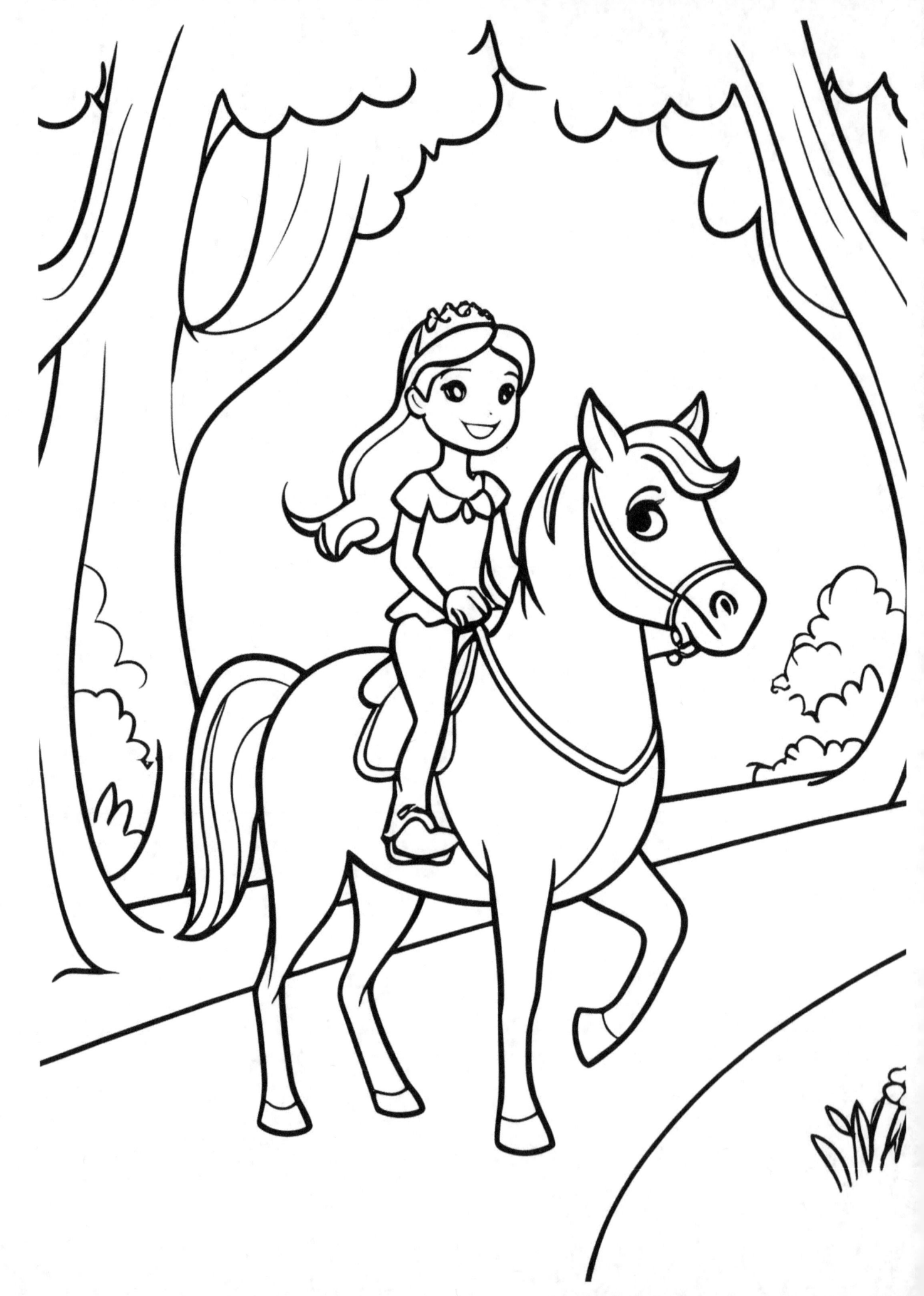

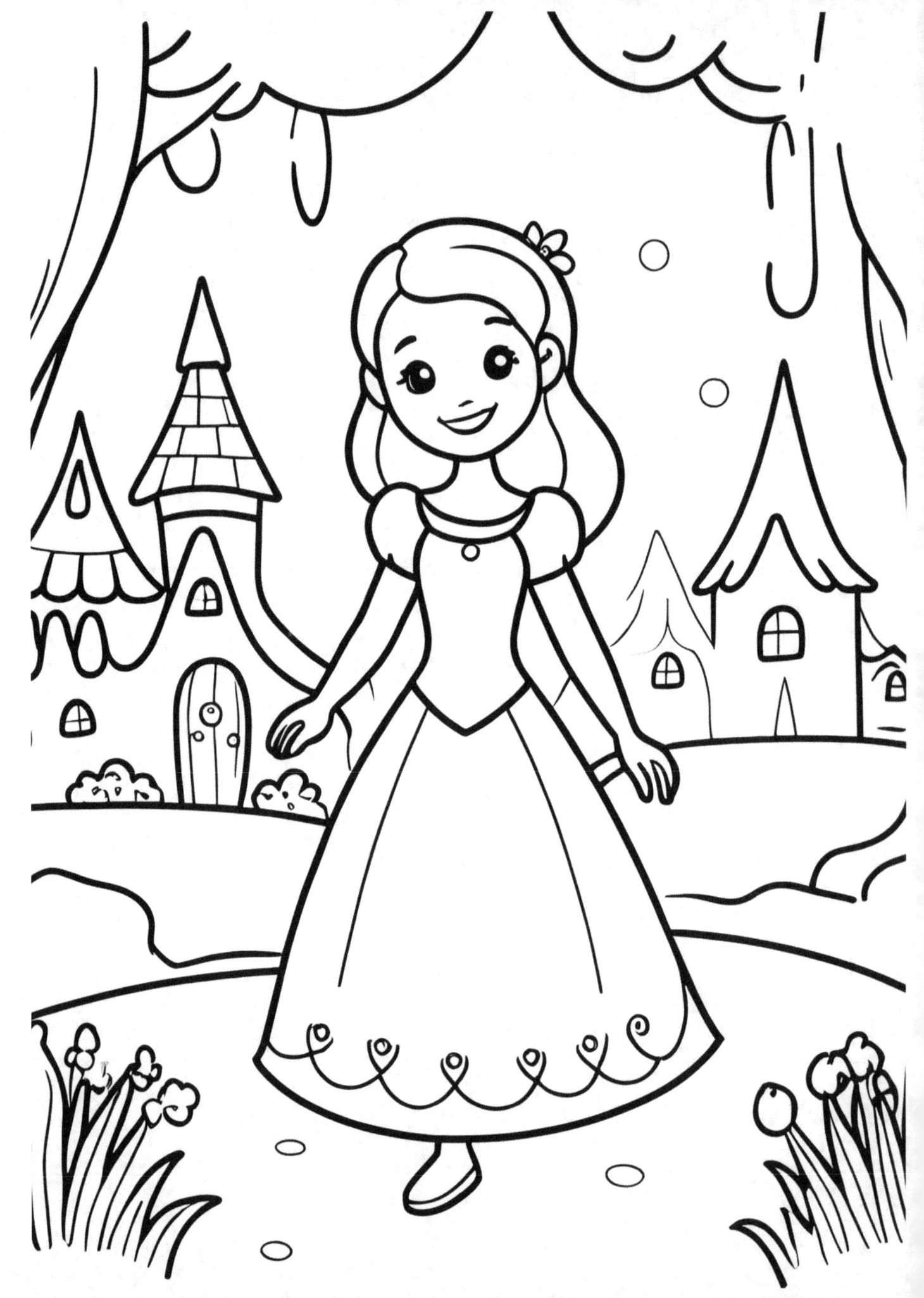

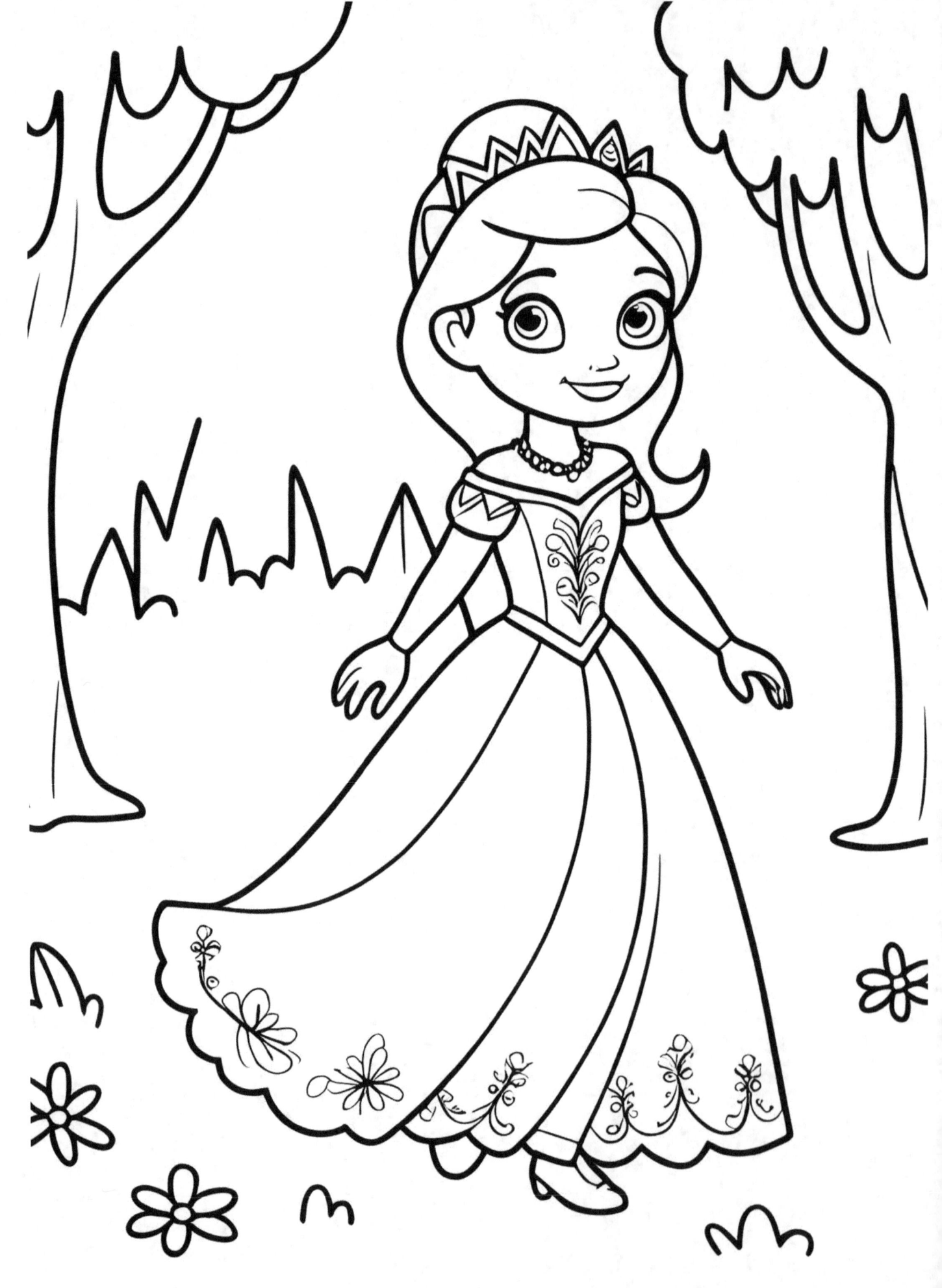

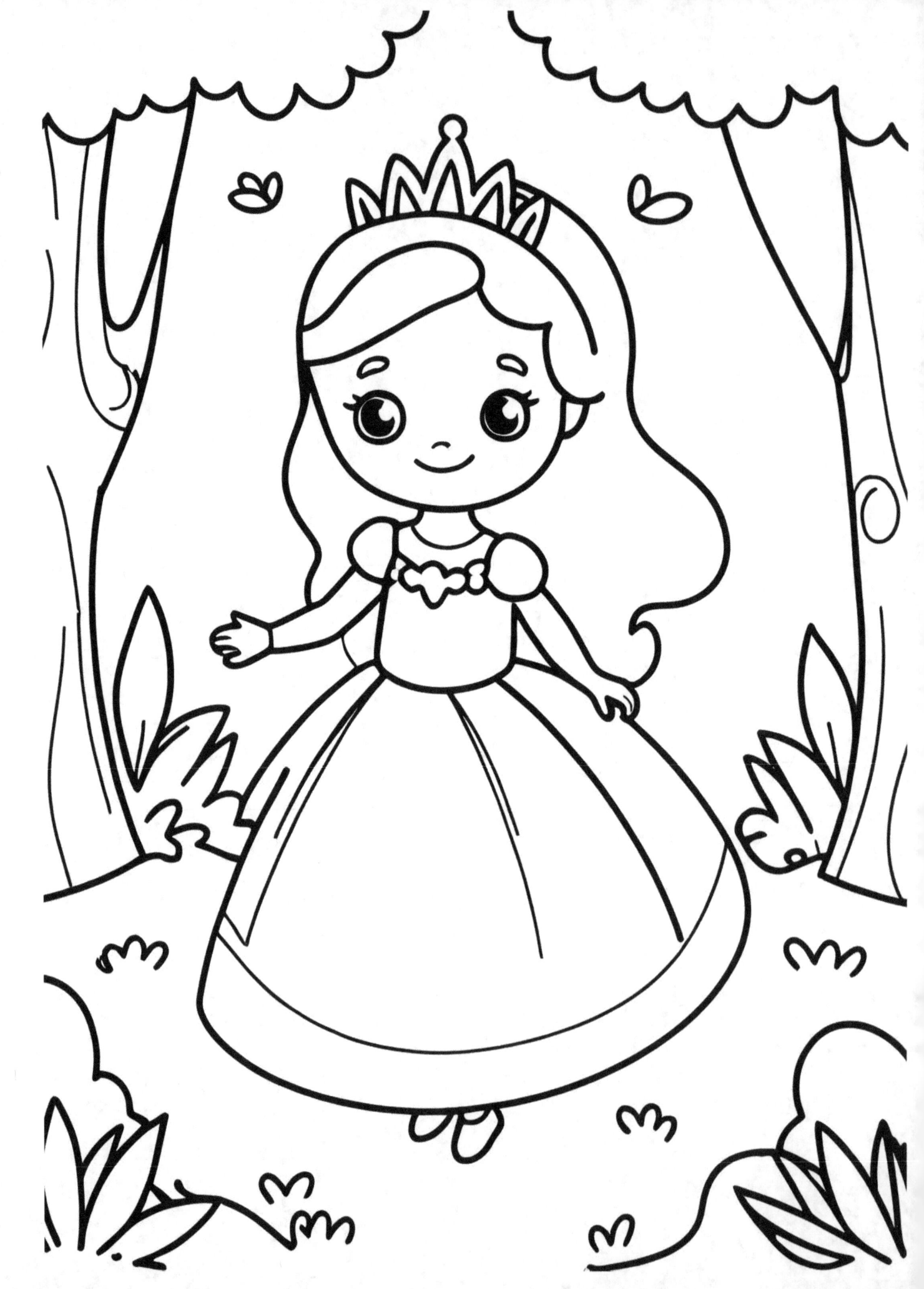

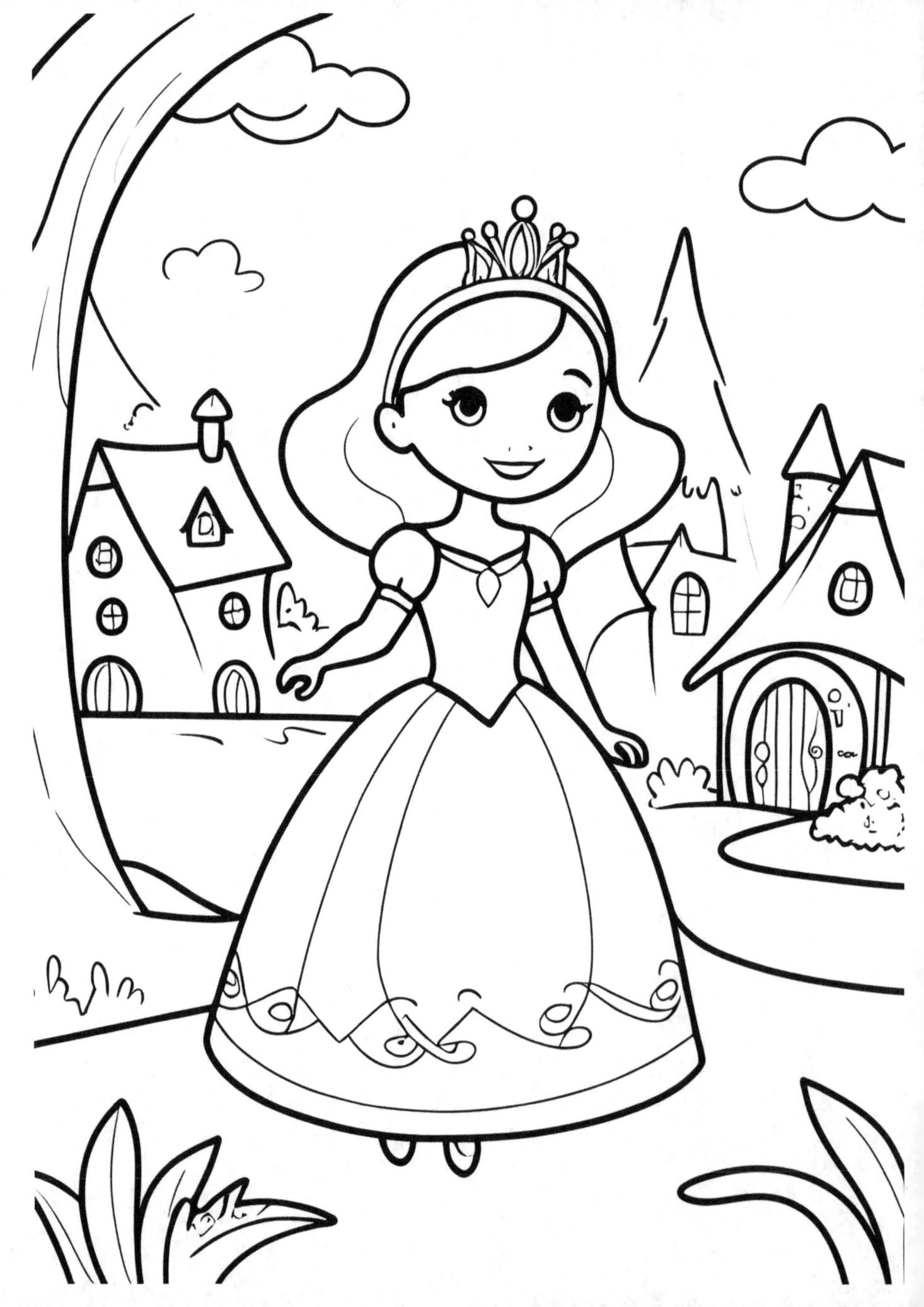

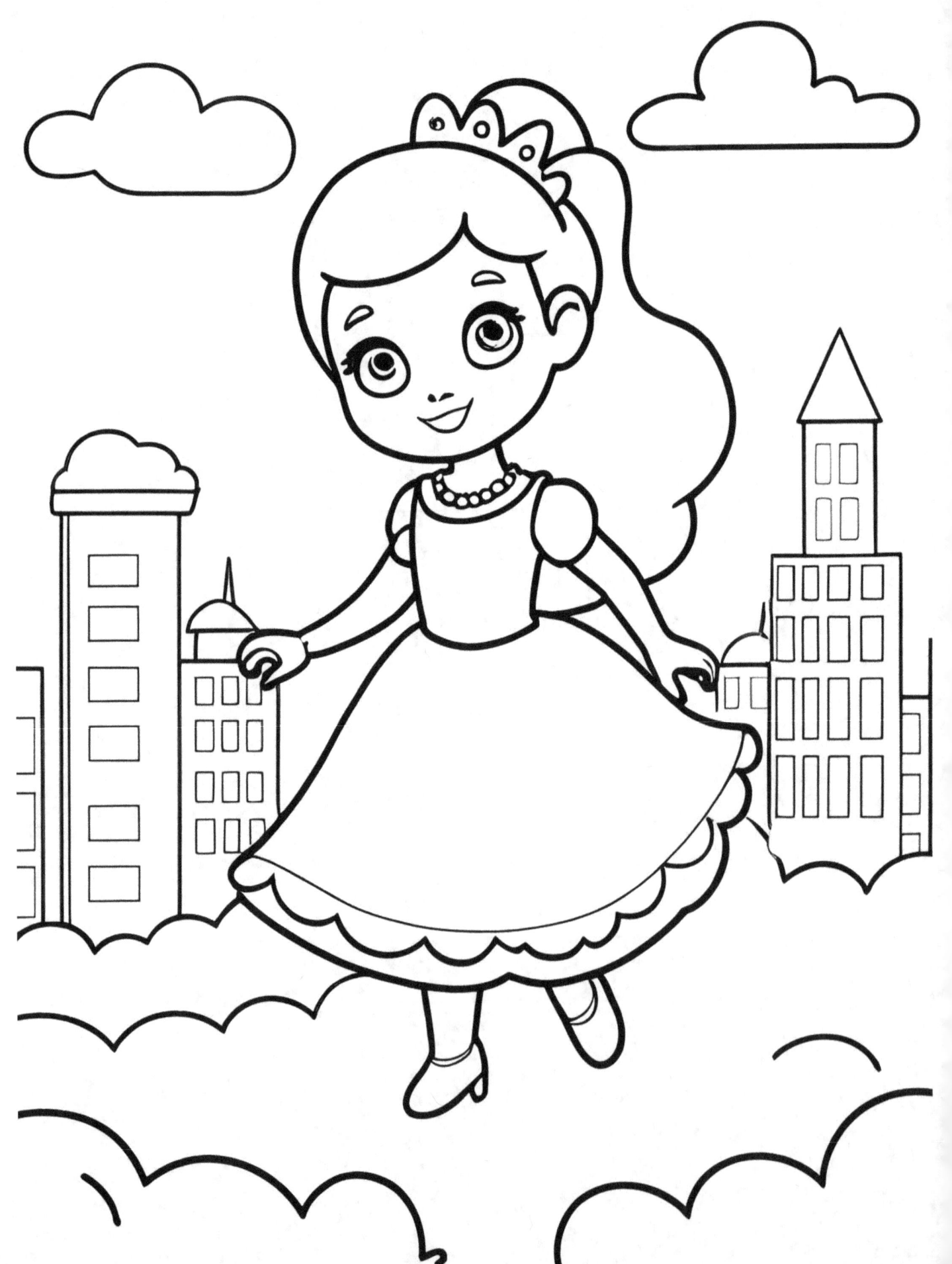

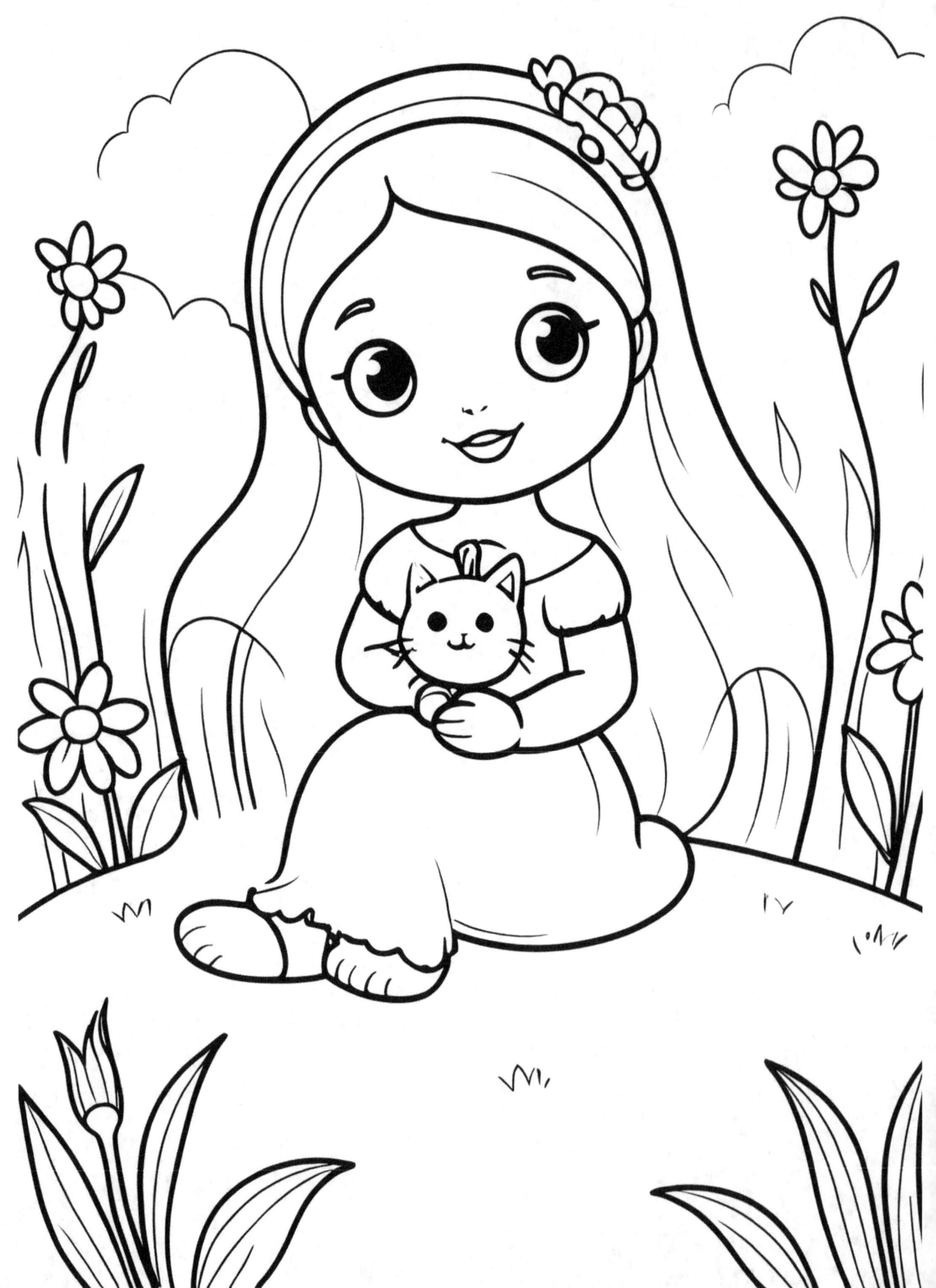

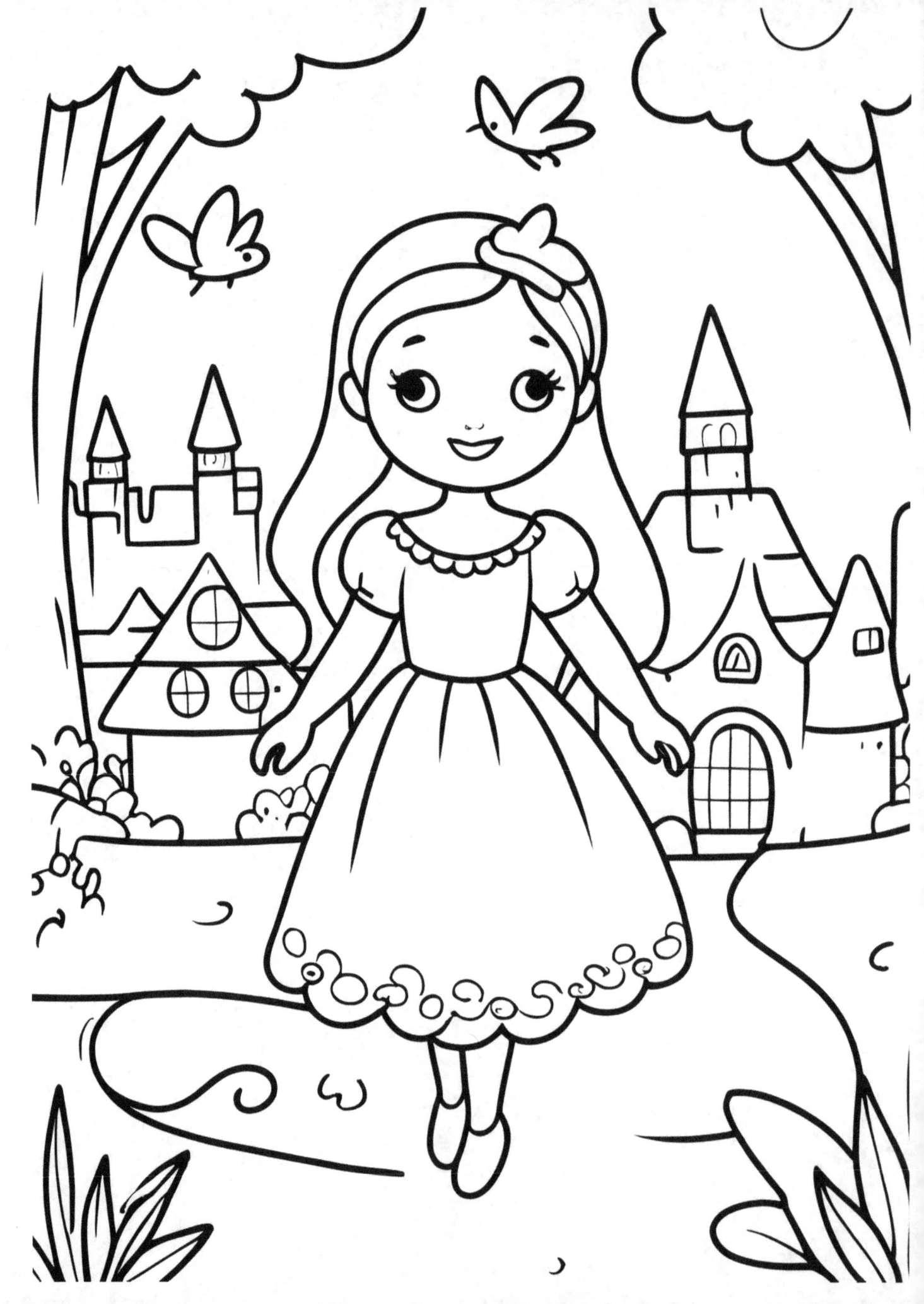

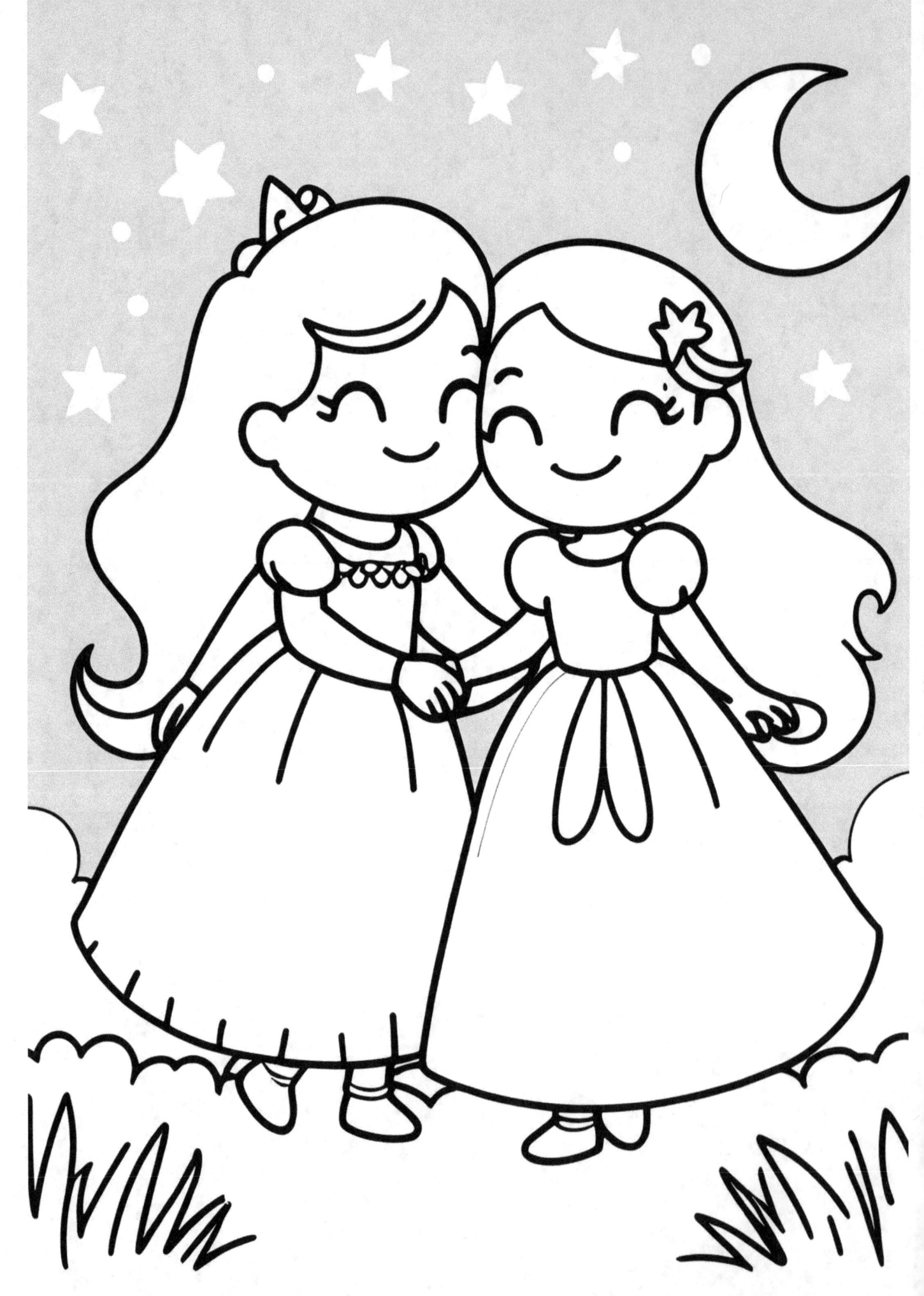

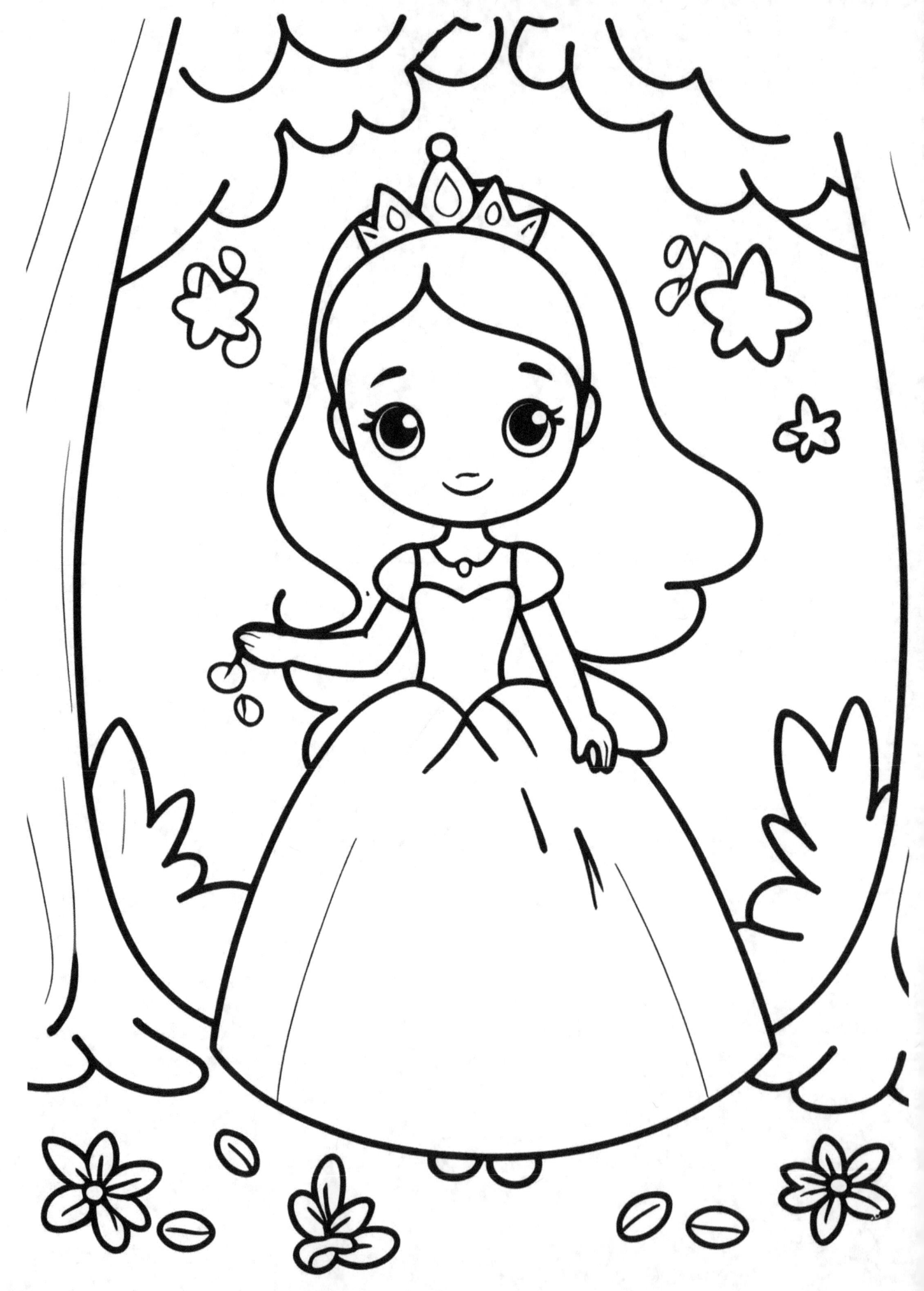

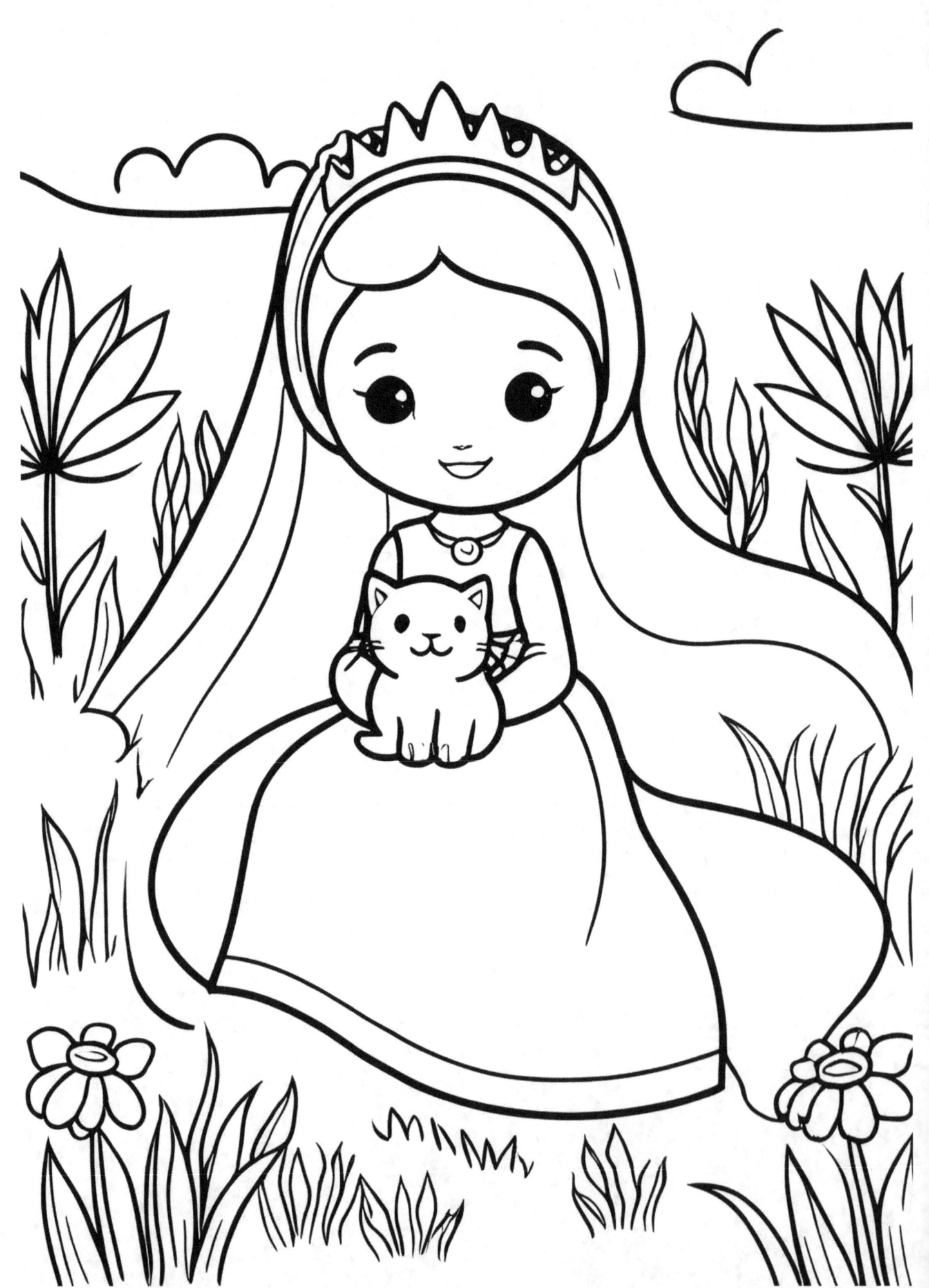

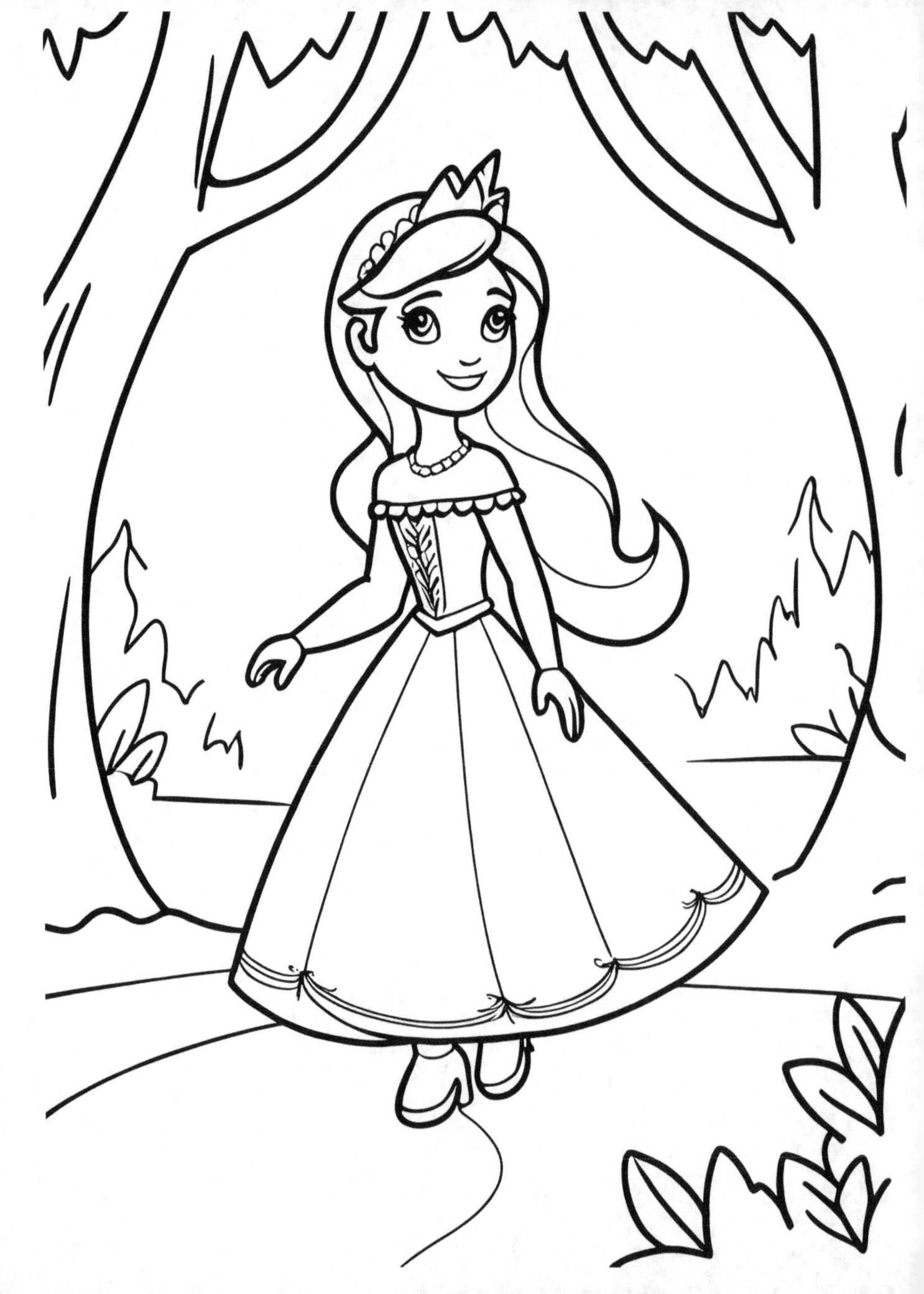

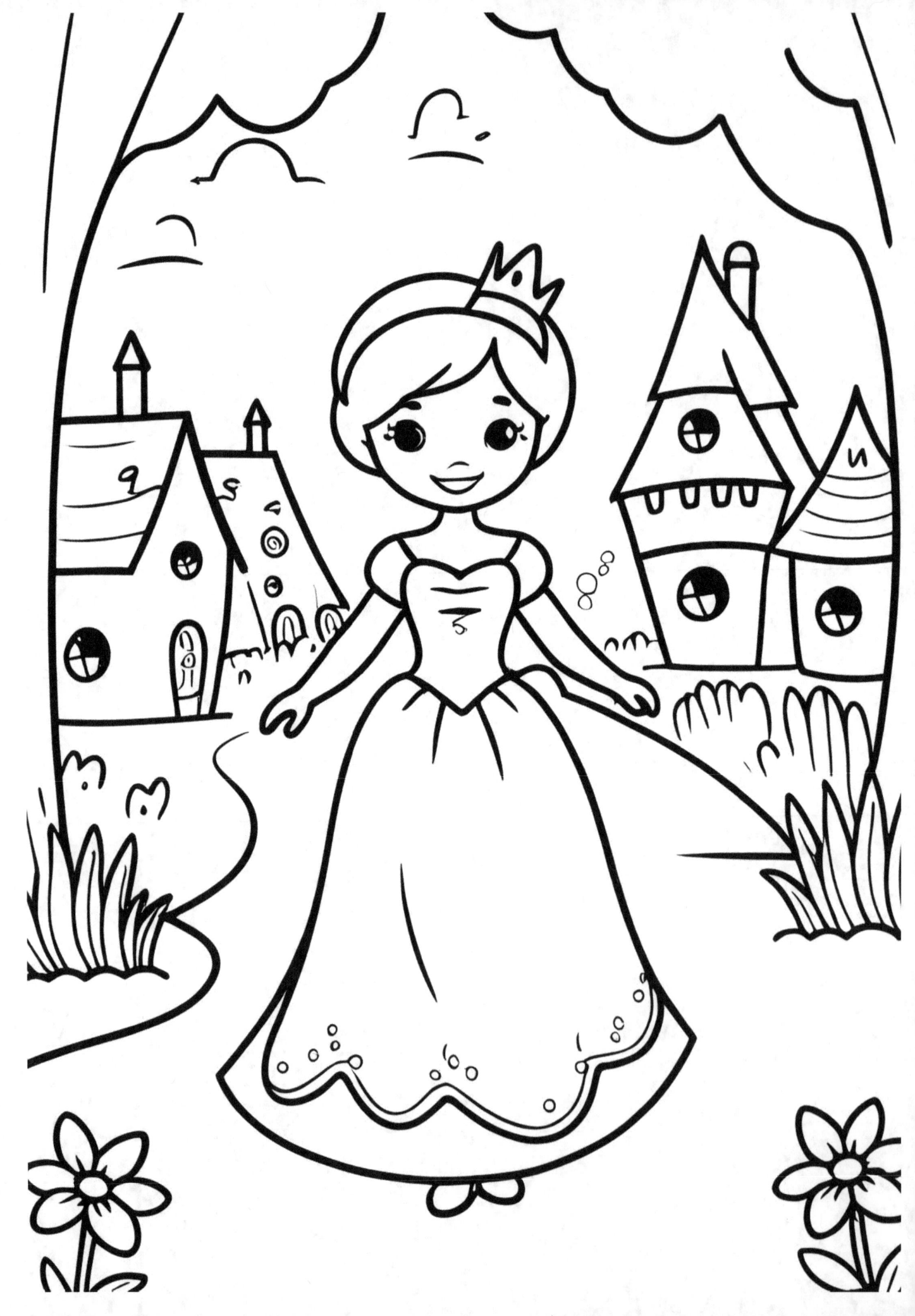

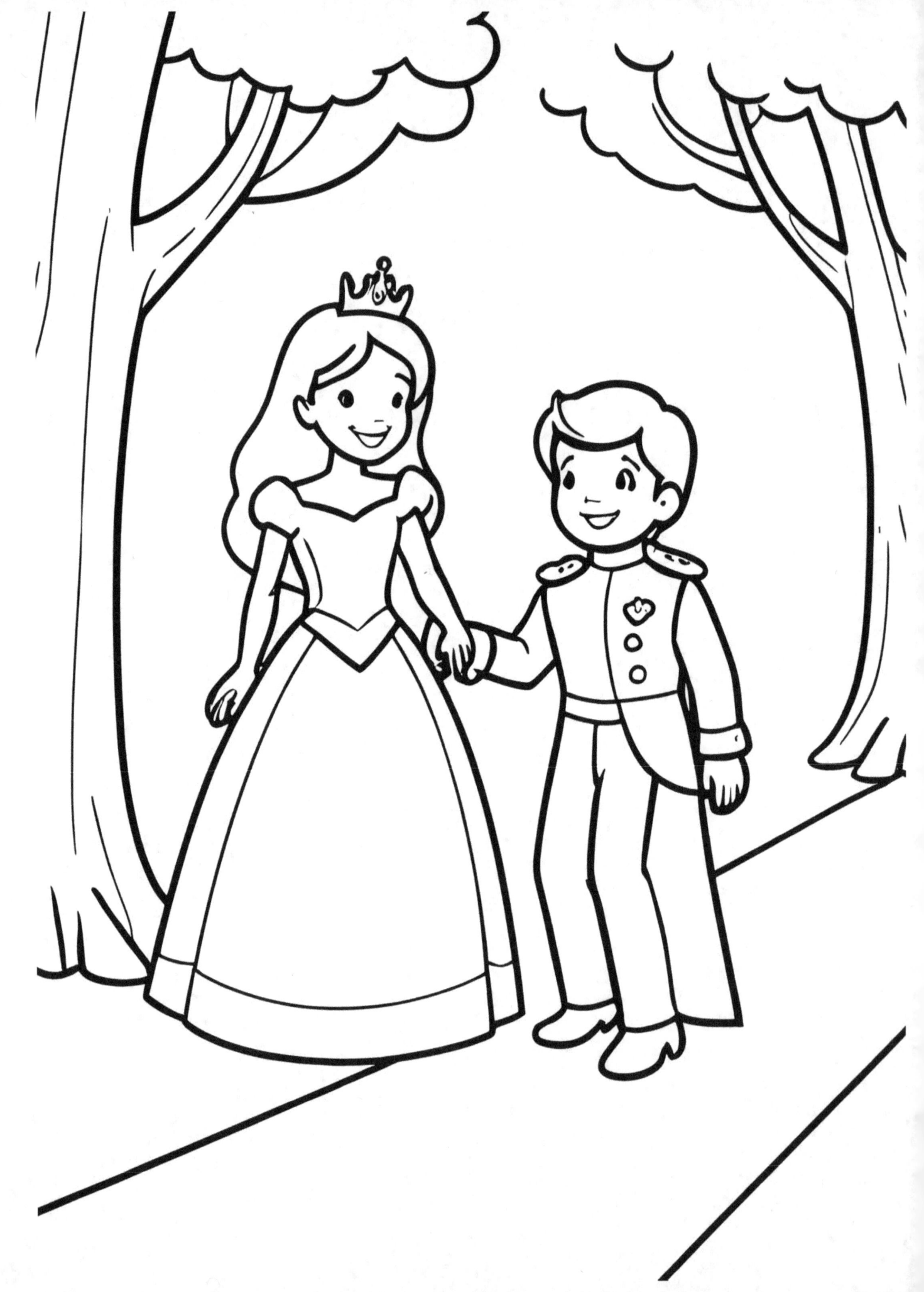

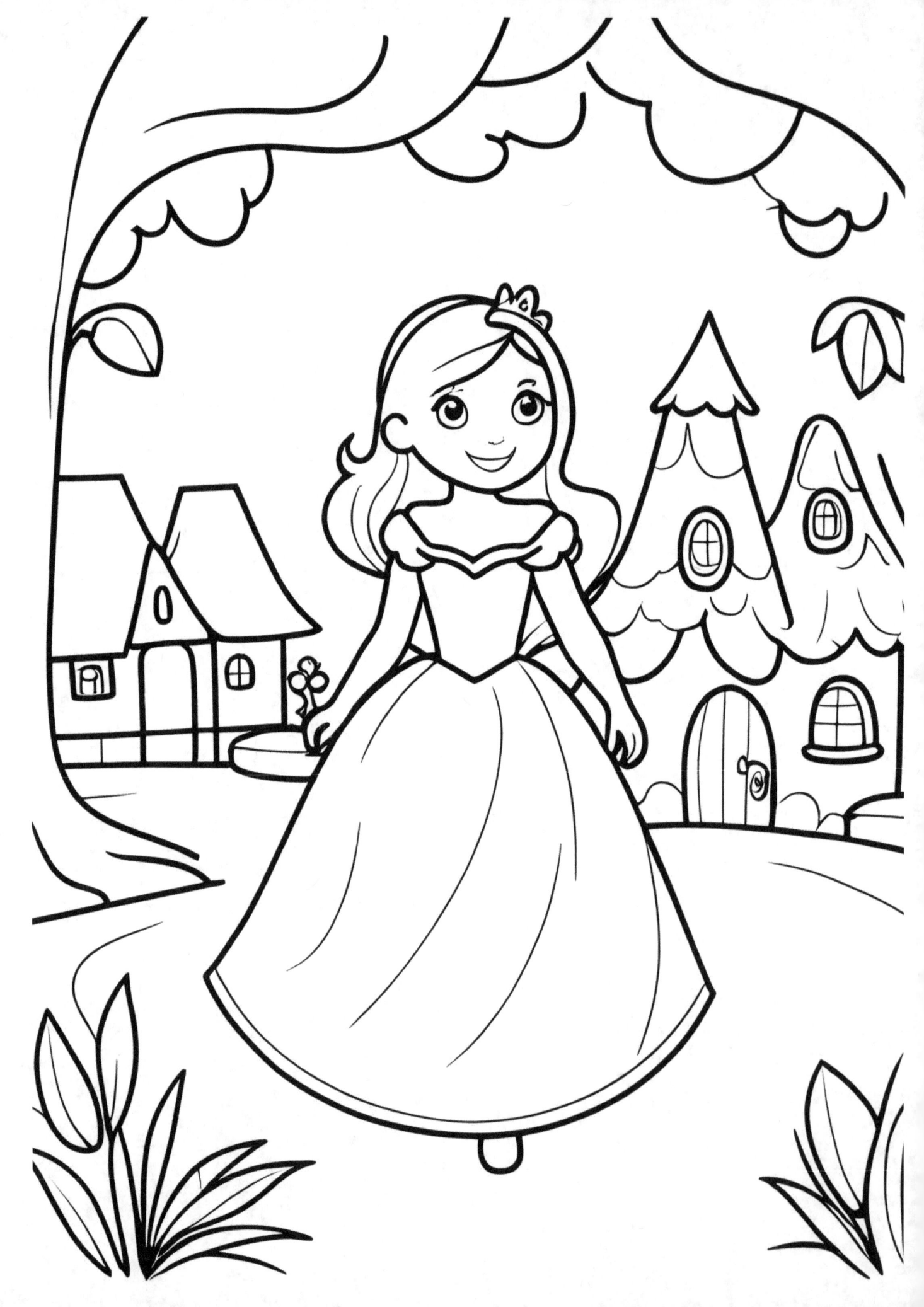

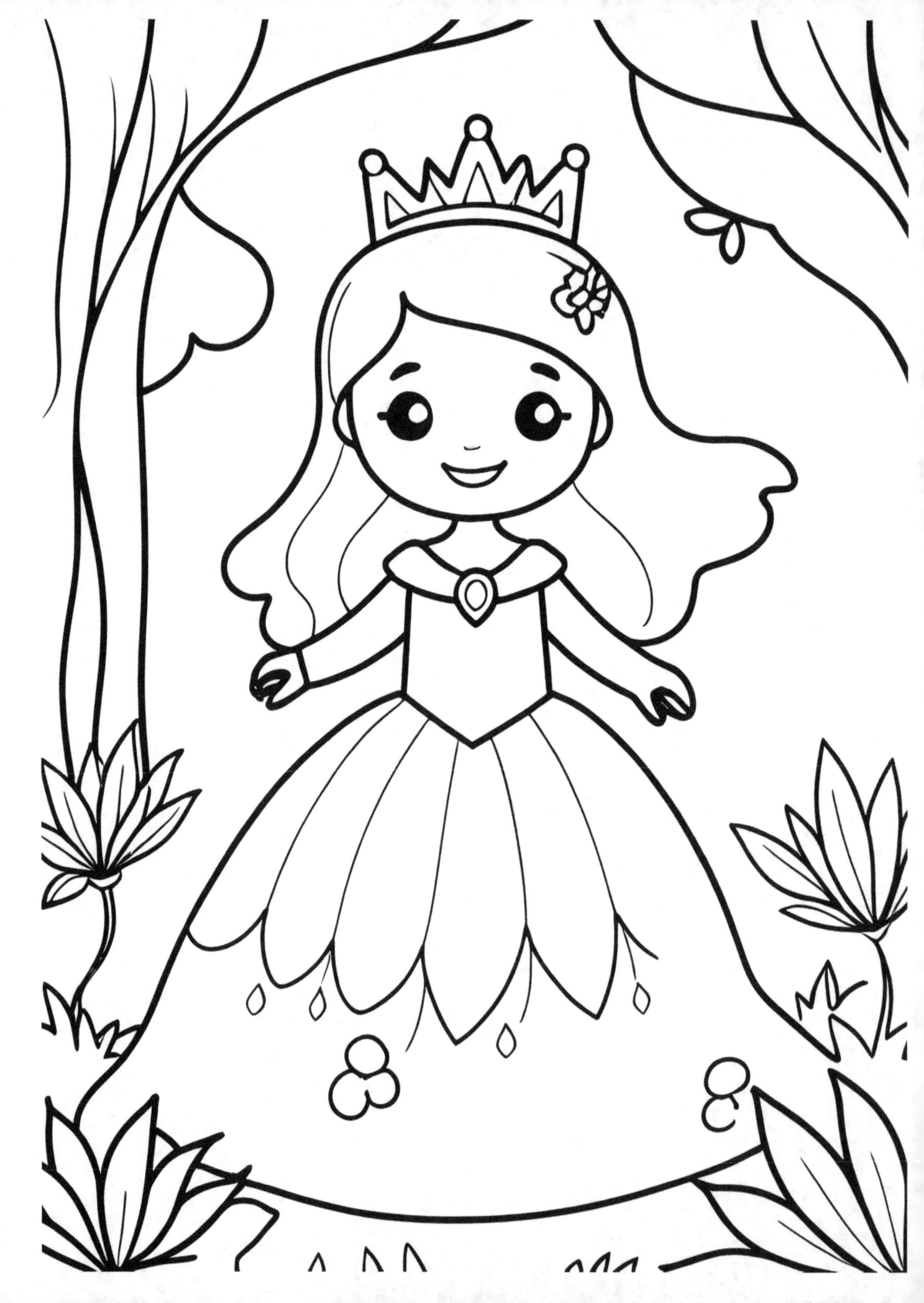

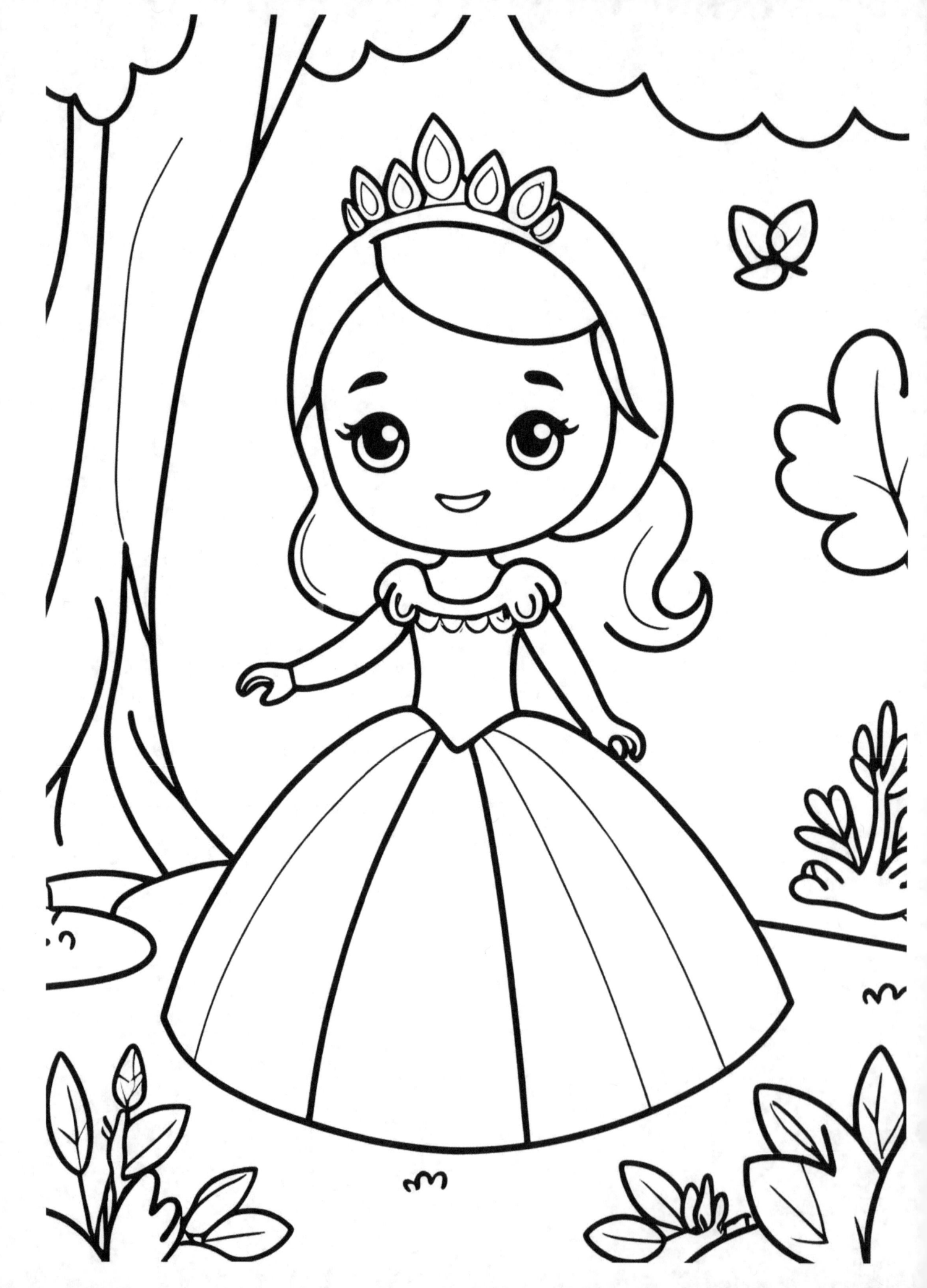

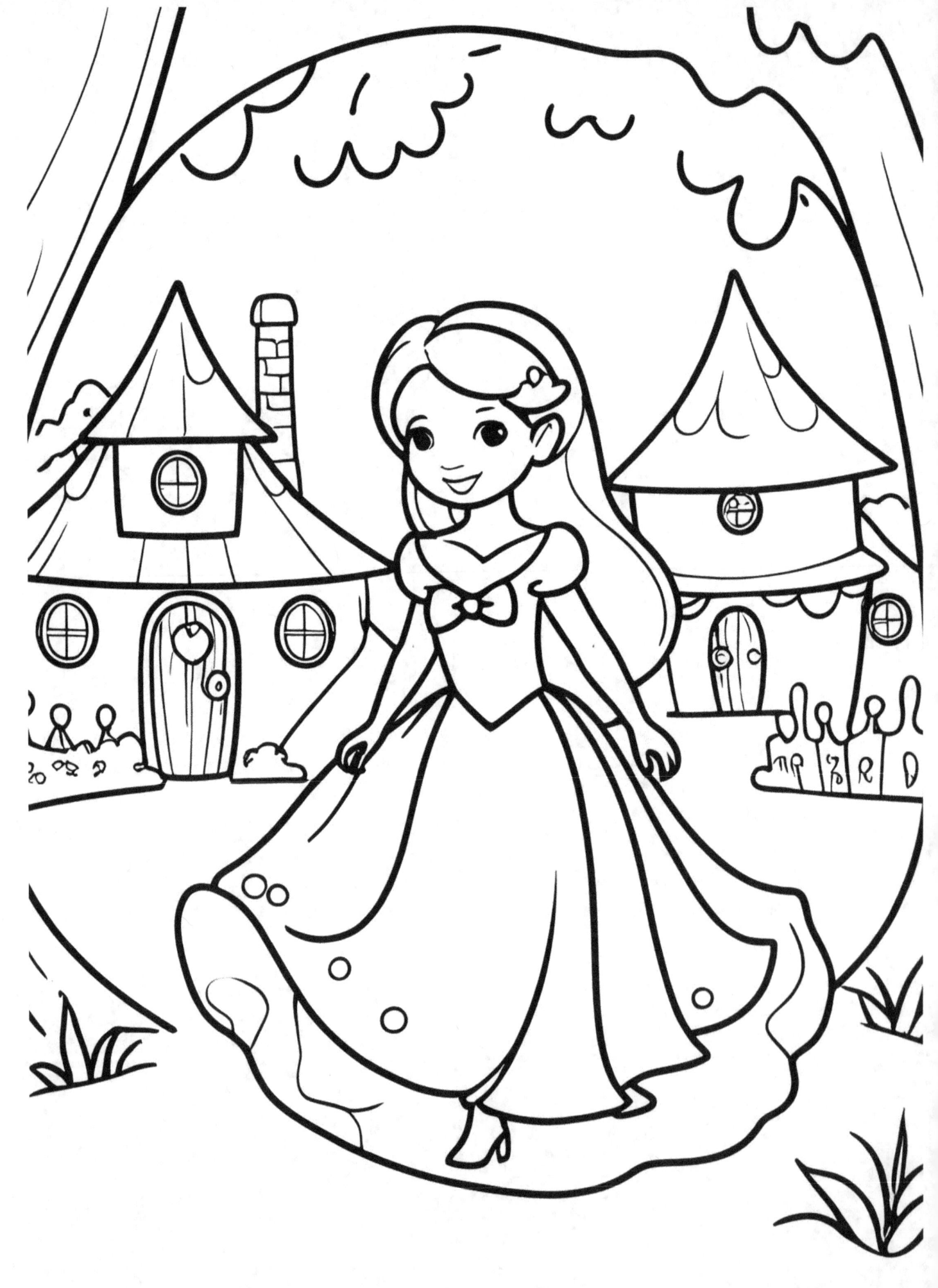

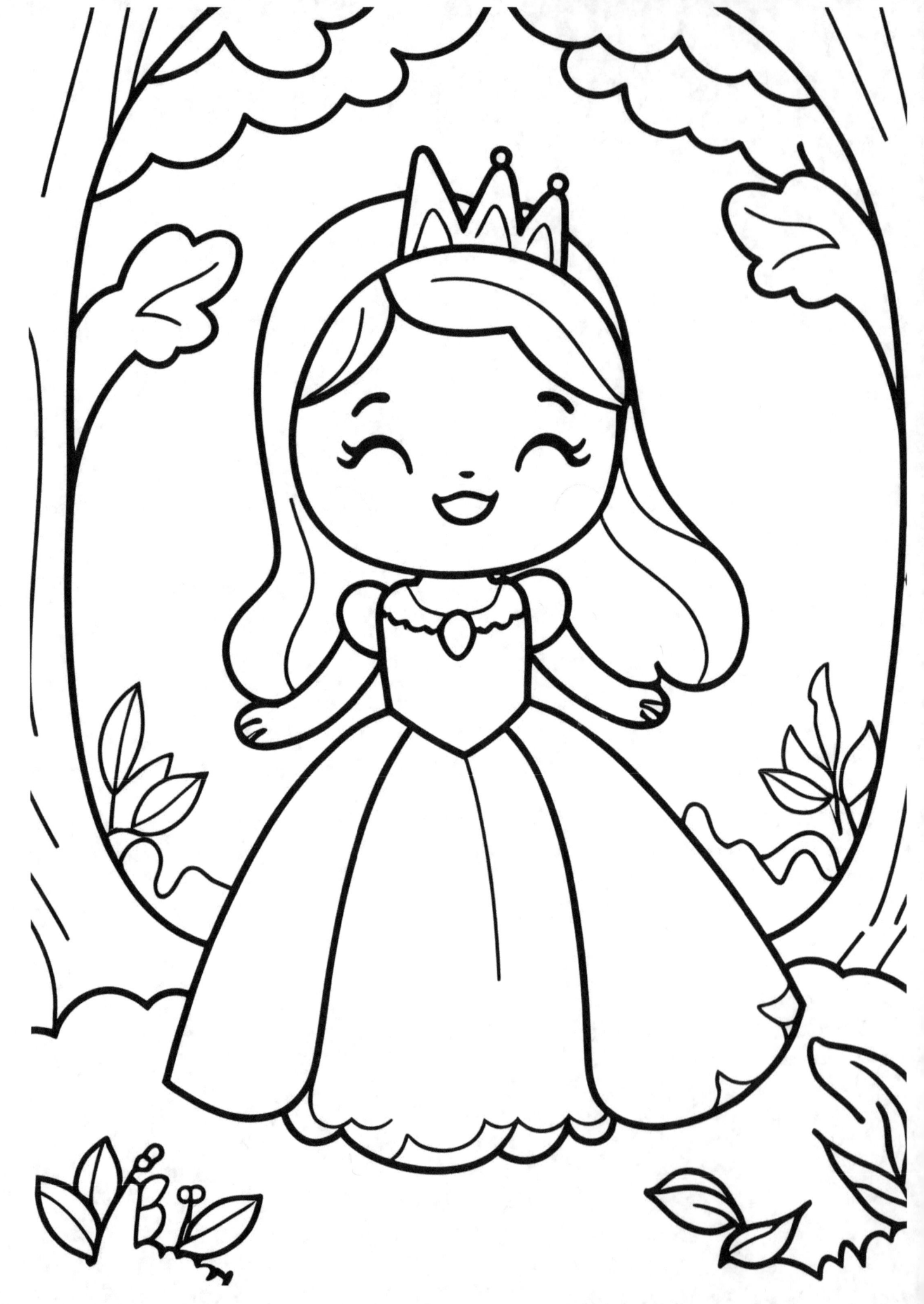

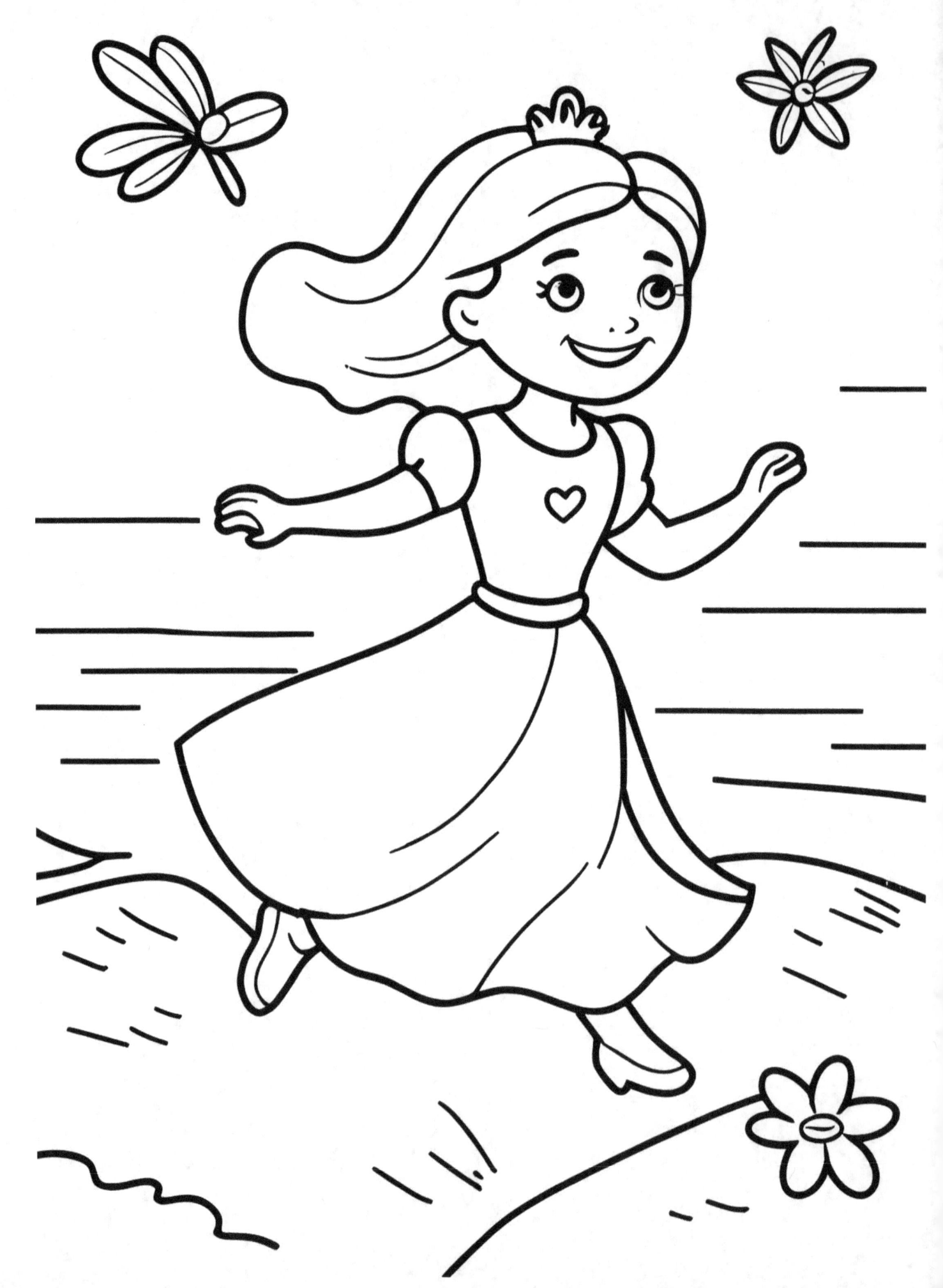

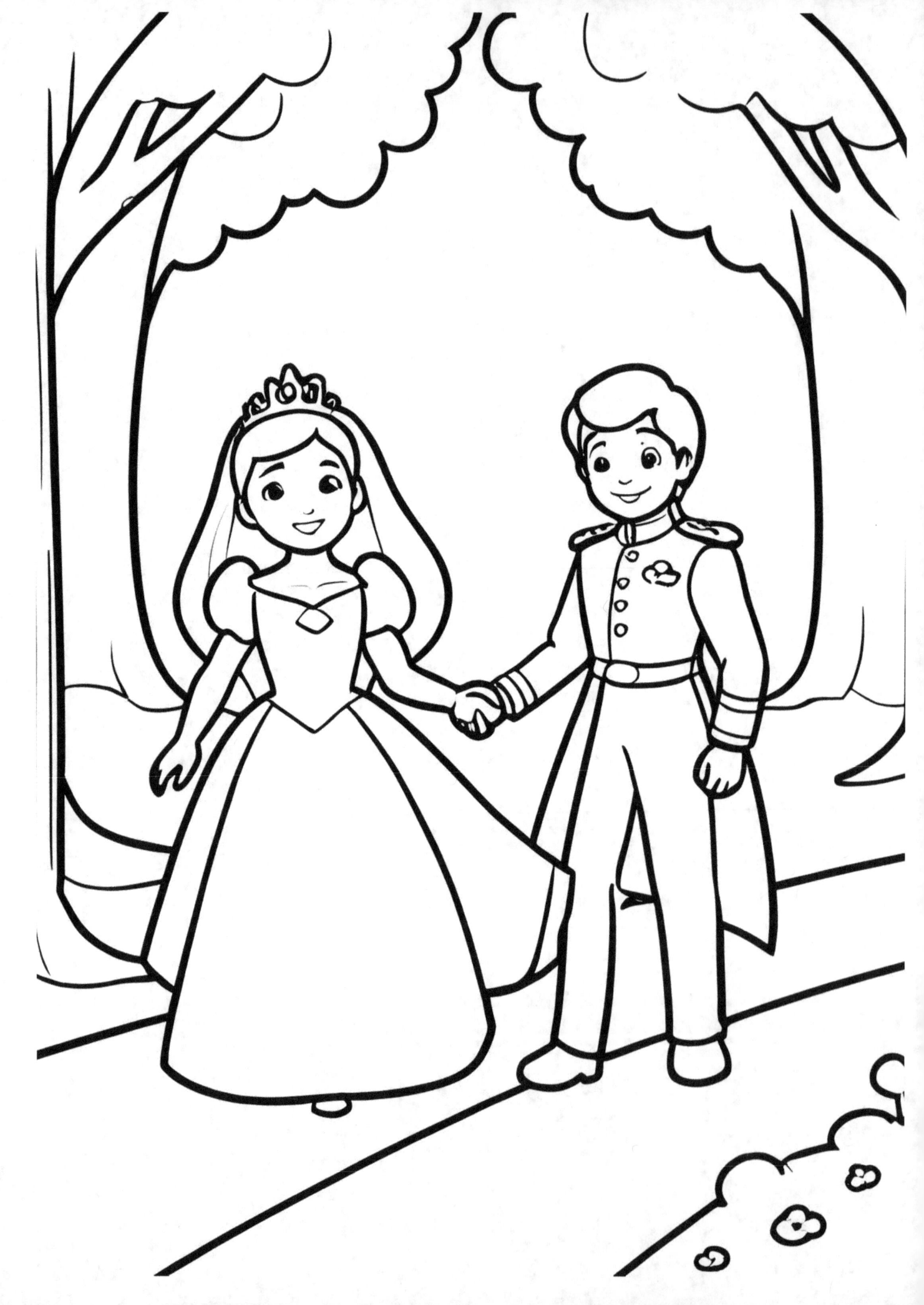

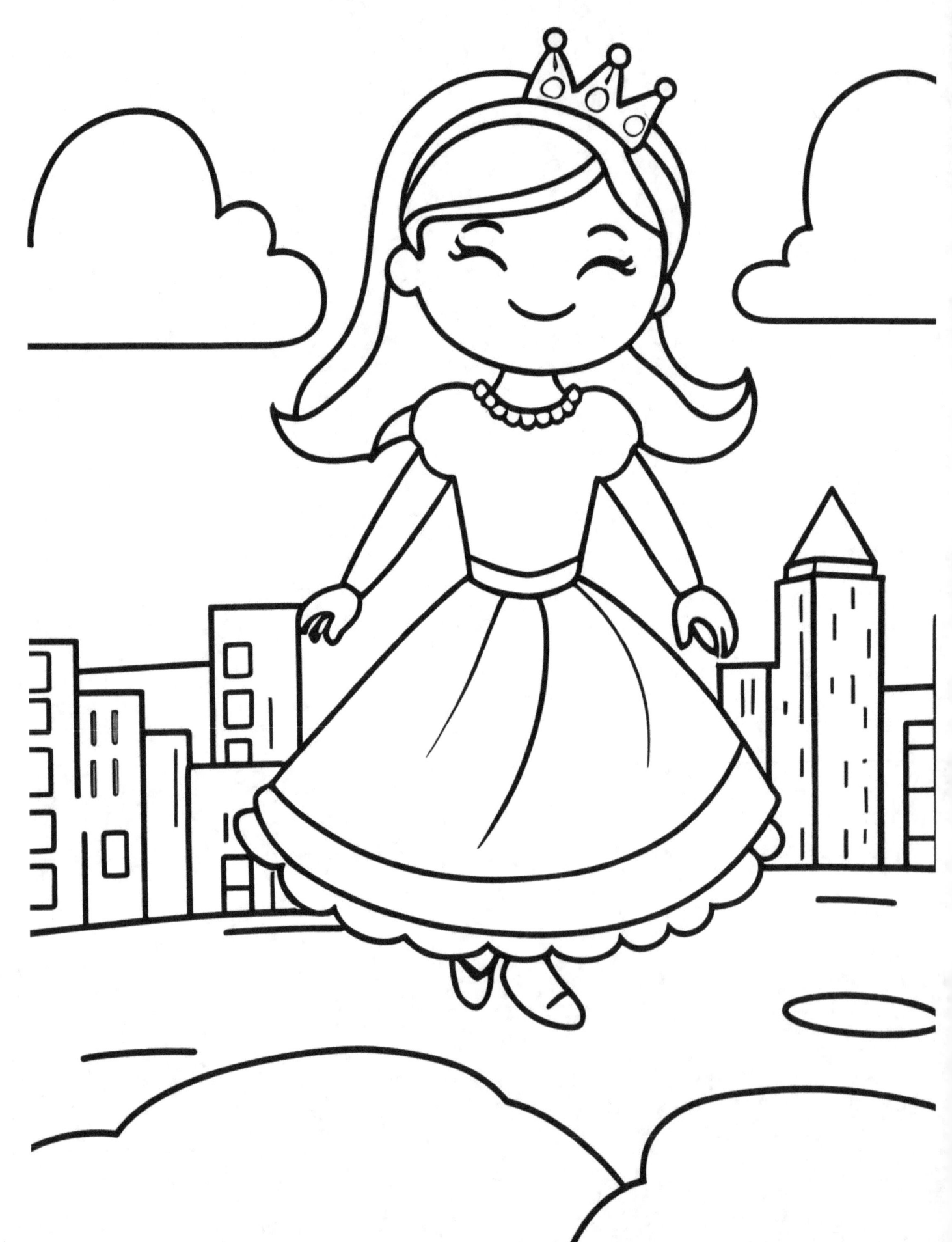

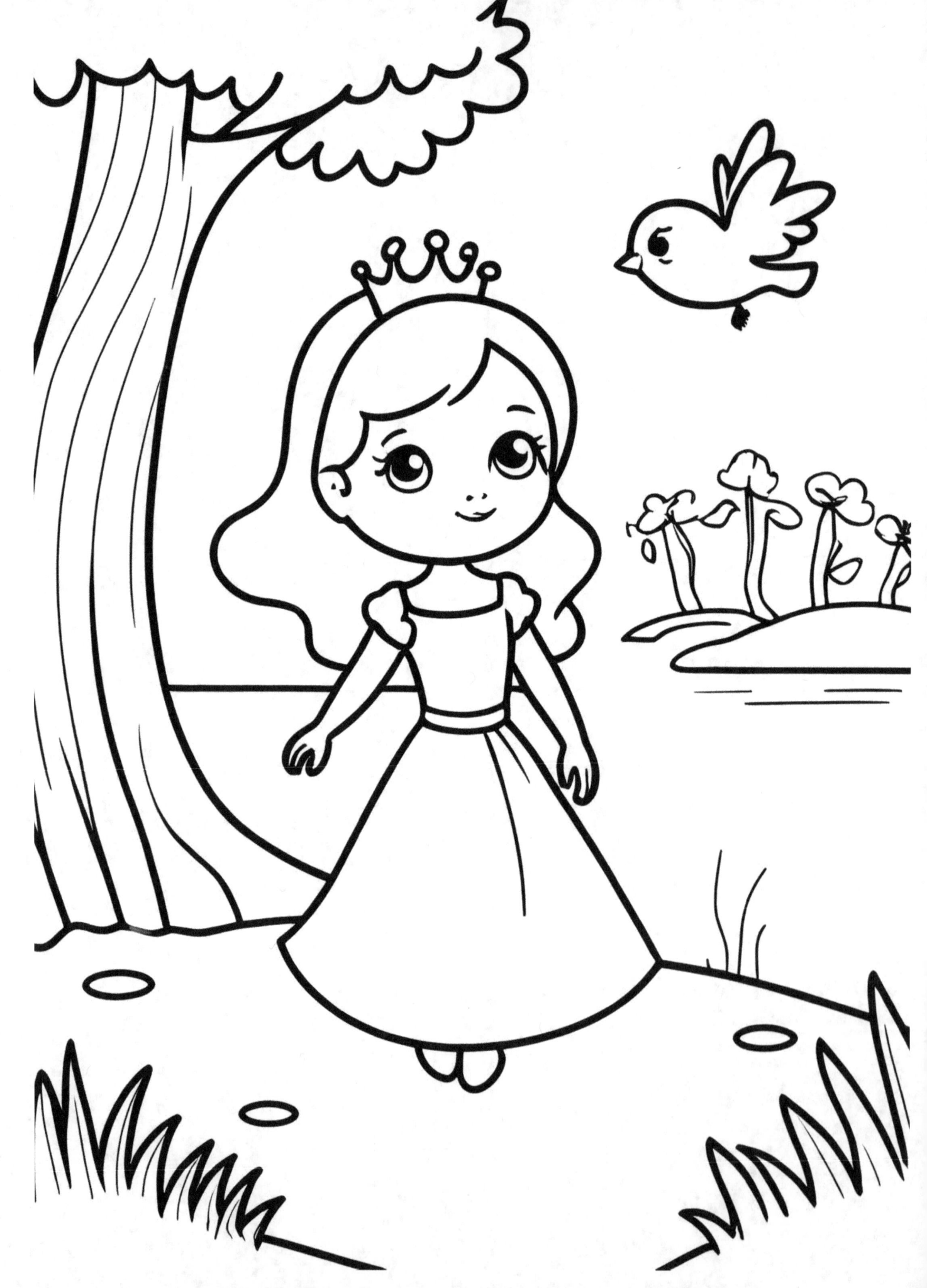